Best Log Home Plans

Best Log Home Plans

Robbin Obomsawin

Gibbs Smith, Publisher
Salt Lake City

First Edition

06 05 04 03 02   5 4 3 2 1

Published by
Gibbs Smith, Publisher
P.O. Box 667
Layton, Utah 84041

Orders: (1-800) 748-5439
www.gibbs-smith.com

Edited by Suzanne Gibbs Taylor
Designed and produced by Modern Grafik
Printed and bound in U.S.A.

Library of Congress
Cataloging-in-Publication Data

Obomsawin, Robbin, 1960–
Best log home plans / Robbin Obomsawin.
— 1st ed.
p. cm.
ISBN 1-58685-146-2
1. Log cabins—Designs and plans.
2. Architecture, Domestic—Designs
and plans. I. Title.
NA8470 .O25 2002
728.7'3—dc21

2001007443

Contents

Acknowledgments 6

Contributors 7

Introduction 9

The Romance of Log Building 10

Everything You Ever Wanted to Know
About Log Building But Were Afraid to Ask 13

The World According to Carpenters 24

Understanding the Design Process 29

Customizing Floor Plans to Fit Your Dreams 34

Expert Tips, Hints, and Techniques 39

Building for the Future 46

The Designer Series Stock Plans 48

Whistling Crow .50

Camp Firefly .54

Star Gazer .58

Birch Hill Lodge 62

Bear Creek Lodge 66

Bluegrass Ridge 70

Lime Hollow .74

Deer Valley .78

Sweet Grass .80

Eagle's Nest .84

Coyote Run .88

Acorn Ridge .90

Forest Hill Camp 92

Love's Cove .94

Turtle Hill Camp 98

Red Hook Bluff 102

Moonlight Bay 106

Celtic Twilight 110

Whispering Pines 114

Wolf Lodge .120

Moss Hill 124

Sugar Bush .128

White Pines .132

Apple Wood .136

Truckee Lodge 140

Nickels Pond .144

Cabin-on-the-Meadows 148

Log Element Outbuildings 150

Saltbox Garage 152

Carriage House Garage 154

Resources 158

Acknowledgments

I appreciate the public's overwhelming support of my first book, *Small Log Homes*. Your enthusiasm and passion for a more thoughtfully planned, conservative form of home has been quite an inspiration to me because I thought I might be the only one in the world with small wishes and big dreams.

I am grateful to my editor, Suzanne Gibbs Taylor at Gibbs Smith, Publisher, for believing in me on a subject that is contrary to the usual "standard" in today's market of home building. I appreciate her foresight, open-mindedness, and willingness to support me in a project so complex and to guide me with her magic pen to make it all appear so simple.

To my husband, Jules Obomsawin, for assuming more of my tasks in our log business over the last few years to enable me to have the additional time to write about and photograph our log-building adventures. His talent and dedication as a handcrafted log builder and husband and father have not gone unappreciated.

To my three sons, Jimmy, Jarred, and Jasson Obomsawin (for whom many of you have expressed concern for their being raised by wolves mentioned in my first book), who have made it through many wild things in life and have grown to be almost normal. I will always love them . . . as long as each becomes a log builder, architect, or engineer! From a young age, all three of my sons have spent hours of their time writing and rewriting many of my thoughts, ideas, and dreams of log building. I am grateful for all their behind-the-scenes help. An extra thank you to my oldest son, Jimmy, who has spent years helping on photo shoots, sharing his wizardry in computer technologies, and bailing me out of many tight deadlines.

To my sisters-in-law Marion Dickerman and Lizza Obomsawin, who have taken time from their busy lives to help me rewrite sections of the book that needed more clarity to express thoughts on a subject that could otherwise be very dry and boring. I am very appreciative of their willingness to always lend a hand when needed.

To my brother Randy Whitman, whom I seldom get a chance to visit, as we both have inherited a workaholic gene. I know that someday, maybe in our rocking chairs, we will have the chance to catch up on old times— perhaps needing the assistance of good hearing aids to converse. With his scientific mechanical experience and my woodworking-design skills, we might come up with a rocker that could keep the blood flowing forever!

To my parents, Jim and Esther Whitman, who have often taken time from their already-hectic business schedules to assist me with editing. I am also very grateful for my mother's artistic influence and my father's creative gift with words.

The most respect and appreciation goes to all of our parents and the generations before them and to those who have worked diligently over their lifetimes to blaze a path before us, enabling us the freedom and choice in life to accomplish whatever we dream.

Contributors

So much work, thought, planning, and so many people are necessary to build a book. I would like to say a special thank you to those who took the time to share their many years of experience in log home designs and photographs to create Best Log Home Plans.

Beaver Creek Log Homes

35 Territory Road
Oneida, NY 13421
www.beavercreekloghomes.com
(315) 245-4112
Beaver Creek Log Homes has been building handcrafted log homes since 1978 and has now turned years of experience into creating specialized log home stock plans.

Beth Singer/Maple Island Log Homes

Beth Singer
25741 River Drive
Franklin, MI 48025
Photo credits: front cover, 8, 49, back cover (upper and lower right)

Fairmont

Le Château Montebello

392, rue Notre Dame
Montebello, QC J0V 1L0
Canada
www.fairmont.com
(800) 441-1414 reservations
All historic photographs are courtesy of Fairmont, Le Château Montebello. The largest historic log structure in North America, built for royalty and dignitaries in 1930, is now open to the public as a five-star hotel and restaurant, with endless activities on-site. Le Château Montebello is a world-class resort overlooking the Ottawa River in Quebec, Canada.
Photo credits: 28, 33, 44

Jean Steinbrecher Architects

Jean Steinbrecher, AIA—Principal
P. O. Box 788
Langley, WA 98260-0788
jsa@whidbey.com
Steinbrecher's log homes showcase her natural talent for design, texture, and balance. Jean's carefully considered and artfully designed plans are true classics. She has been designing homes since

1972 and specializes in many forms of log home and commercial structures.
Design credits: 120–23, 140–44, 148–49

Maple Island Log Homes

5046 SW Bayshore Drive, Suite A
Suttons Bay, MI 49682
www.mapleisland.com
(800) 678-0175
Maple Island Log Homes has been designing and building log homes since 1977. Their photographs illustrate many of their unique design ideas for a number of their special clients.
Photo credits: ii, 8, 11, 38, 40, 41, 42, 43, 45 (upper right), 49, 151, front and back covers.

Nickels Design

James Nickels, Architect
P.O. Box 636
Victory Hill
Victory, VT 05858
(802) 695-1071
James Nickels has been designing log homes since 1963. His classic New England–design style maximizes the space and budget available.

Nickels Design specializes in many forms of log homes and commercial structures.
Design credits: 110–13, 128–31, 132–35, 136–39, 144–47

Roger Wade/Maple Island Log Homes

Roger Wade
P. O. Box 1130
Condon, MT 59826
Photo credits: 38, 41, 43

Trout House Village Resort

9117 Lake Shore Drive
Hague, NY 12836
www.trouthouse.com
(800) 368-6088 reservations
Some of the design ideas within this book were based on the Trout House's rental cabins, built and refined over generations. Trout House Village is located on Lake George in upstate New York's breathtaking Adirondack Mountains. This popular all-season resort is a great place to rent a cottage and catch the vision of how a log home should feel.

Introduction

There is a depth of passion experienced in log building that touches our hearts and captures our souls. The warmth and simplicity of wood enrapture us, bringing out the pioneer spirit in all who appreciate the timeless look and rustic charm of a log home naturally in balance and harmony with its surroundings. We celebrate the beauty and embrace the small imperfections of natural logs that, when touched by the hand of a log craftsman, are transformed into works of art.

As our world spins faster through more complex technologies, we long for our home to be a refuge in which to think and dream. In this high-tech world, we want to appreciate the simpler things in life, and therefore prefer a less-processed look. We admire the rustic character of a log home, but want to combine it with modern conveniences.

This log home collection features classic designs from three of the top design professionals who specialize in log home construction methods. These popular log home designs preserve the look and spirit of the traditional craft of log building, which is devoted to the use of natural materials, classic designs, and fine craftsmanship.

I have had the advantage of living in many houses over the past twenty years because our clients provide a place for our work crew to stay while we are building their log homes. I am often invited into homes all over the world, as others want to share with me what they have created, pointing out the things they love and things that still need more work. Seeing a variety of home layouts has given me the chance to study what works well and what does not. It has taken years of experience and planning to create a collection of log homes that is not designed for the industry or the paid advertiser but for those eager to build something classic in design and detail, something beyond the standard construction drawing and the average floor plan—something different from the ordinary. Each stock plan has been thoroughly checked by qualified log builders, assuring that the designs are workable in the world of handcrafted log building.

Since we do not want to waste our natural resources, we carefully review each and every plan and make sure we maximize every square foot. The inspiring combination of natural wood, stone, and glass gives an extraordinary feel that passes beyond the four walls of the home to share with all who enter.

From a wide choice in a diversity of styles, we hope one of these homes might fill your family's needs and inspire you to incorporate a few favorite design ideas, creating a log home that captivates you not just for today, but for generations to come.

The Romance of Log Building

Romance has long been the driving force of every person with passion, and there simply is not a more romantic home than a log home. The same holds true for the process of building a log home. The romance of handcrafted log building is done with a passion where even the smallest detail is carefully and thoughtfully considered. The desire is to create a sculpture that is an extension of the earth, disturbing nature as little as possible. Romance is found in building a log home that captures a spark of magic, takes one's breath away, yet intertwines with

an element of surprise that mesmerizes all who enter.

Romance has inspired American creativity for generations and has kindled many dreams. Vision and ingenuity is expressed in the home through texture, color, light, scents, and sounds, all of which stimulate an atmosphere of romance. The blending of these elements creates a home that reflects individuality and interest in life. To capture this romance requires research, hard work, planning, and discovery. Now more than ever in today's complex world of endless choices, intense focus is required to achieve both function and beauty.

Mastering the world of handcrafted log building demands patience and dedication. Logs are a living, breathing element with natural dynamics and properties that are not familiar to many people today. Many of the materials used are raw, organic substances,

requiring the owner's and builder's reverence, respect, and knowledge of the power and capabilities of Mother Nature. For those who relish the raw beauty of nature, it is pure inspiration to walk through the forest and find the materials needed to create the sculptural elements and special details that bring a home to life.

Since years of experience are needed to master this art form, the prospective buyer reaps great value for the amount of hours, skill, and artistry invested in a handcrafted log structure. Although rustic in nature, it is far from unsophisticated. Many of the tools still used in constructing a handcrafted log home are quite primitive, but by adapting new technologies, handcrafted log builders are able to produce complex structures well beyond the range of what our ancestors envisioned.

The romance of building is often overshadowed by the reality of the cost and

complexity of today's construction technologies. It is sometimes hard to remember that the enjoyment is not just in the completed project but also in the journey of design and the process of building. It is a fantasy dreamed of by many—a home built with care by one generation, to be passed on and enjoyed by one's children and grandchildren.

It is the greatest dream realized when you can look upon your completed log home and know that all your hard work and vision have been transformed into a magnificent storybook design that will continue to provide the ultimate romance, now and forever!

Everything You Ever Wanted to Know about Log Building
But Were Afraid to Ask

Over years of talking to log home enthusiasts, contractors, architects, and engineers about building log homes, I've found that everyone asks the same types of questions. The following list of the most frequently asked questions do not have in-depth answers, and some issues will require more information and details, depending on specific needs.

What type of wood is best for log building?

We often get hung up on the "perfect" wood species and forget about the capabilities of the craftsperson. You can have the best species of wood to work with, but if you do not have a good builder, the type and quality of wood will not matter. The secret to finding the best wood is to choose a better builder—it is then that you will

end up with a great log home.

There are many types of wood that are perfect for log building. Experienced builders understand the individual characteristics of the woods being used. There could be varying combinations of woods chosen based on many factors, such as structural properties for the roof type and expected roof load, wall spans and floor joists, insulating factors, and the woods' availability. Experienced builders will choose the best wood for the overall design.

There are a great many species of wood found throughout North America, with some of them being the best species in the world for log building.

Isn't it easier to build a log home than a stick-built home?

No. There are many factors in log building that are complicated by the natural dynamics of whole-log construction and its out-of-the-ordinary joinery methods, such as allowing for shrinkage of logs around doors, windows, and fireplaces; calculating the various sizes and locations of mortise-and-tenon and round-on-round log-joinery connection points; and determining allowances needed for plumbing, electrical, and heating chases.

To build a log home, the basic skills of conventional construction must be used and understood, along with additional knowledge of special log-building construction methods. A builder and homeowner must respect

and understand the special considerations of building a log home. In my previous book *Small Log Homes: Storybook Plans & Advice*, there are two full chapters dedicated to these special needs, along with a checklist for contracting a log home. It is important to understand these unique considerations when planning and constructing a log home, even if you are not doing the hands-on work yourself, so you will not meet with unexpected difficulties. The informed consumer will be better prepared for the journey ahead and left without a bitter pill to swallow at the end of an unsuccessful project.

Do log homes last as long as stick-built homes?

Yes. There are handcrafted log homes in Europe that are six hundred years old and still standing. They all have some basic things in common, such as large roof overhangs and off-the-ground foundations. Initial construction was done by knowledgeable and skillful craftsmen, and the structures were well maintained over their lifetime.

Do log homes cost more to heat than stick-built homes?

No, not if they are properly built. Log homes are very cost-effective to heat because of their thermal mass, which is naturally formed air pockets created by the cell structure of a log. When a log home is not energy-efficient, it is almost always due to one of four reasons:

The thickness of the log walls is too small. The smaller the diameter of the log, the less insulating value and overall thermal mass it will have.

The log construction has inferior joinery due to the builder's substandard construction methods, lack of education, and/or experience.

Contractors or sub-trades do not respect the shrinkage details required in a log home, which in time can create "wall hang-ups," allowing air infiltration.

There are many specific design features that push up the heating bills. Some examples are high or vaulted ceilings, fireplaces, oversized windows, and other areas in large and expansive-style homes.

Should I hire a contractor or do the work myself?

Building a home is a large undertaking. If you underestimate the time frame or needed skill of a project, it can have a devastating impact on the budget and/or the project's outcome. Evaluate how much time you have to dedicate to your project. Building a home is a full-time venture, requiring a full work crew for at least six months or more in order to complete a small or average log home. This does not include the time spent in constructing the log shell. If you do not have a large block of time and a full work crew, and if you lack personal experience, it would be best to consult a professional.

The general contractor oversees the specified work and quality of the application. It is hard to know what to oversee if you do not have a good knowledge base of the trade. The subtrades may find it frustrating and unproductive to work with an owner who does not understand the sequence, time frame, materials needed, or lead times necessary for the project. An experienced tradesperson may charge additional fees for a project that is overseen by a greenhorn or novice supervisor, as he or she realizes that loose ends and poor coordination will create an inefficient project that is likely to be drawn out over a long period of time. When a project loses momentum and focus, things start to become much more work than they are worth.

If saving money is the only reason for doing the job yourself, then you may want to reconsider building your own log home. If you shop around for professional help, you might find that the professional's expertise may save you more money (and definitely more frustration) in the long run than if you build it yourself.

Another important advantage in hiring professional tradespersons is that they are more likely to be licensed and insured. A tradesperson is responsible for problems that may occur once a job is finished, including improperly installed plumbing, improperly engineered floor joists and roof support, or insufficient shrinkage details. As a homeowner, you may not be covered by insurance if a project you were unqualified for backfires.

I have some cracks in my log walls. Is this going to compromise the structural integrity of my home?

No. Changes in the temperature and humidity of the logs cause checking (cracks in logs). This is a natural occurrence and is considered part of the appeal and charm of a log home. This natural process of checking does not compromise the structural integrity in any way if engineered properly. However, stress fractures may occur when there is an engineering defect. These are much larger in size and are often caused by an excess of weight in one specific area. Stress fractures may develop if undersized logs are used in load-bearing points, if logs span too long a distance without vertical support, or if improper joinery is employed. Consult a specialist if you are not sure of a situation.

Why is there shrinkage in a log home?

Shrinkage and settlement occurs with time and is created as the amount of moisture in the logs drops. Even though the individual logs do not shrink significantly, the overall shrinkage of all the logs in a wall is considerable over time and affects the wall height. Compression is also a factor caused by the weight of the materials, which creates an additional decrease in the overall wall height.

Logs do not shrink measurably in length, only in circumference; therefore, only the wall height is affected. This process occurs most significantly during the first five years, but does continue throughout the life of the home. Shrinkage and compression are considered part of the natural dynamics of whole-log construction.

A general rule of thumb is that for every foot of log-wall height, there is a ³/₄-inch allowance for shrinkage. This allowance must be made to accommodate the shrinkage that will take place around the windows, doors, chimney, plumbing, and conventional walls. Extra space should be included around these details and filled with insulation that can be compacted over time. Trim boards are attached to cover the insulation, which can be removed and adjusted whenever needed.

The idea of shrinkage and settlement sounds complicated. Do I have to allow for that much room?

Yes. Settling is only a problem if you do not allow for it. As logs shrink and your windows and doors do not, you may find yourself with cracked windows and doors unable to open if you do not allow for enough shrinkage. Or you may find your plumbing buckling and your second-floor toilet base raised five inches off the floor! Once your builder has calculated how much extra space you will need, be sure to allow for at least that amount. For example, if your window is four feet high, the allowance above the window would be calculated at three inches (4 x ³/₄ inches). Do not try to "save yourself work" and only allow for two inches. The amount of work required to create a three-inch space is no greater than to create a two-inch space. You will save yourself a great deal of time, money, and frustration if you carry out this critical procedure. The design detail of shrinkage is not hard or complicated for an experienced carpenter; it only becomes difficult when ignored.

There are those who try to find wood that is very dry so they do not have to deal with shrinkage. Handcrafted log homes have been built with green logs for hundreds of years; the shrinkage detail is a simple and natural part of this type of construction and is feared

only when not understood. Ninety percent of handcrafted log homes are still built using green wood. If dried wood is used, one must consider the expansion of dried logs as they absorb moisture in high humidity, in addition to some shrinkage and compression. Even a kiln-dried or standing dead log will expand as well as contract as an ongoing natural process. Every log home will settle and have shrinkage, whether green or dried wood is used.

its stick-built cousin, the standard of which is a three-bedroom home with no fireplace, eight-foot ceilings, and primarily of wallboard construction; whereas the standard log home often has vaulted ceilings, stone fireplaces, tongue-and-groove ceilings and walls, wood flooring, stone tiles, and so on. There is no longer a fair comparison.

In handcrafted log homes, the consumer often wants a log home that has more specific ideas of design details than the conventional-home consumer. The log home today is often far from generic. To incorporate character and detail can make a home come alive, converting a humdrum home into a jewel. One must realize, however, that adding character and incorporating special touches has a price.

How much does a log home cost to construct?

The magic answer is . . . well, there is no magic answer. This is the most-asked question in all types and forms of construction and the hardest to answer. It is like going out to buy a car and asking how much do all cars cost per square foot or how much per pound. The cost of both conventional 2 x 6 construction and log home building depends on the quality of finished materials intended for use, along with the chosen builder's experience. Factors that affect the cost of construction are closely tied to the scope of a project—level of quality materials, design details, combinations of specifications, and economic conditions of the region where the home is being built.

The only way to get an accurate bid is to have precise construction plans that fit your needs. Many construction plans are very vague in specifying building materials and methods, which in turn can make it difficult to get an accurate bid. Because many plans are so vague, the homeowner is left unprotected, and the trades have an open-ended contract

How does the cost of a log building compare with a conventional stick-built home?

Pricing a log home cannot be based on conventional methods, as it is not a conventional form of building. A general rule of thumb is that a log structure runs a third more than a conventional structure. Keep in mind that most people tend to compare the log home to and choice of materials or methods to be used without a set level of quality standards being determined.

The construction plans are the largest part of the contract between you and your builder. These are very different than floor plans as seen in floor-plan magazines and books. The floor plans and the elevations give the homeowner an idea of the layout and overall look or façade of the home, but the floor plans are only one-fourth to one-third of the information included in full construction plans. A full set of construction drawings gives critical information needed for the builder to make accurate bids, such as construction and joinery details, measurements, specifications, cross-sections, and other pertinent information, making the biggest difference in the overall cost and quality of a project.

Are there any other ways to give me an idea of how much a handcrafted log home will cost, for the sake of a general budget starting point?

One general budget starting point is the "one-third" theory. Take the cost of the log shell and double that figure to calculate the costs for the house's conventional components. Then add the two figures together for an estimate of the total cost. For example, if the log shell costs $75,000, you would double that figure for the conventional components ($75,000 x 2 = $150,000). Added together, the total cost of the log shell and the conventional components will come to about $225,000.

There is a second type of calculation that can be made to estimate a log home's general cost in which the home's square footage is multiplied by $160 (based on construction costs in 2002). For a home of 2,200 square feet, multiply that number by $160 and the estimate is $352,000.

Remember that these methods provide only crude estimates. Even if both of these methods are used to calculate costs for the same home design, the result could be two very different numbers. Other factors not formulated into these estimates are cost of land, long driveways, difficult building sites, very deep wells, unusual or complicated design details, over-the-top kitchens and baths, long-distance deliveries of the log shell, and landscaping.

In more than twenty years of building, not one site or client's needs have been the same, and the word average in building is a very broad term. The above estimates

are a general average and there is nothing average about custom building!

What is the least expensive way to build a log home?

A four-corner rectangular log home is the most inexpensive to build, keeping in mind that nothing in today's market is inexpensive to build. A home's design does not have to be unusual or expensive to create a knockout look. Clean lines and simplicity can be spectacular!

Cost can be closely tied to the design of a home. Dormers, bump-outs, complicated details, and dramatic roof systems all add to a home's cost. Although these things add character and charm, a storybook cottage or cabin without all the bells and whistles can still be achieved.

I want to build a handcrafted log home but cannot afford the style of home I have chosen. What can I do to keep construction costs down and in check to make my dream a reality?

It costs nothing to dream. Having to deal with real costs to make that dream a reality is another story. However, do not let the sting of mortgage payments and the cost of living keep you from fulfilling those dreams. Here are some suggestions for cutting construction costs to help you bring your dream to reality:

- Look for a four-corner building and a simple roof system. Building a home is a series of trade-offs, especially if you are on a tight budget. No matter how many years you put into designing the perfect home, there will always be trade-offs to make, no matter the size of the home.

- Evaluate your needs and wants in a home. Needs are must-have items to function day to day, while wants are luxuries not needed in our everyday lives. You may find that living with less gives you more time to enjoy your surroundings.

- Use a stock plan instead of a custom plan. Stock plans are only a fraction of the cost compared to developing custom plans. If there are only a few items that need to be altered to fit your needs, it is very cost-effective to have the "base plan" customized to fit your lifestyle.

- Use standard stock materials in construction instead of custom materials for items such as kitchen cupboards, window, trims, etc.

- Build a log home with a conventional roof-framing system instead of log components. If planned well in the designing stage, a conventional roof system can flow with the structure instead of appearing disjointed.

- Use drywall in the roof system and dividing interior walls. There is a lot more light reflected with drywall or plaster and it can serve as a great contrast to the natural logs. It is not necessary to have everything in wood in a log home. The logs' greatest complementary materials are textures that give depth to the home's design.

- Do not stipulate a stone foundation if your budget does not allow it. Many log homes do not have stonework in the foundation, only a grey parge finish that was left exposed. Once the grades are formed and a minimal amount of landscaping is in place, the foundation's finish is not noticed.

- Incorporate the garage into the basement. The advantage is that this design hides the mess and clutter that a garage tends to harbor. The tucked-away garage provides a lower profile to the overall structure and therefore will not compete with the house as it would if it were standing next to it.

- Use a pier system instead of a full foundation, crawl space, or slab. Check with your local builder to see if this is feasible for the site location; it can be a big cost-saving option if workable.

Top Ten Biggest Mistakes Made in Log Building

1. *Designing too much home for the budget*—When custom building, it is very easy for things to spin out of control for the owner before he or she even has a clue that it is happening. "Live now and pay later" and "Well, I didn't know" doesn't exempt the owner from the choices made. Overspending or insisting on having it all does not support your dream when you are suffocated by the stress of repaying the debt. Be prepared and informed of the project's cost.

Building a home is a big investment and it takes time to learn and absorb all the information.

2. *Not enough thought and planning before building starts*—Any who have actually been through the process of building know that planning takes a lot of self-evaluation, research, and focus. Detailed thought and planning about each phase of construction, including good construction plans, is critical to a successful project and the realization of a dream home.

3. *Installing the log shell or other natural framing members too close to the ground, even where there is no snowfall*—Another consideration is the splash-back area created by the rain's run-off from the roofline as it hits the ground and splashes back onto siding materials or log work. An exception can be made for a covered porch that has no walls, and can therefore be ground level.

Just remember to include proper post installations.

4. *Building too short of a roof overhang*—Oversized roof systems are more than ornamentation; they are a very important design feature of quality home construction. If the contractor does not have this information clearly marked on the construction plans or tries to build shorter roof overhangs to save cost, then there will be trouble in the long run. Log homes can withstand getting wet, and they actually thrive with humidity, but constant and repeated water saturation shortens the life of any home.

5. *The use of cheap-quality materials*—Low-grade materials stand out like a sore thumb and devalue the appearance of a quality handcrafted log home.

6. *Choosing an inexperienced general contractor or log builder*—Look for a contractor with a solid background in construction, who appreciates and understands handcrafted log homes.

7. *Purchasing the log shell or overall home's bid solely based on price*—Take time to understand the different quality and styles of log joinery. The least expensive bid is not always the best choice, whether in log work or general construction. It is often hard to know how to evaluate an overall bid, but a contractor's experience is very important. So many homeowners base their decisions solely on the bid amount and not on the content and supporting documents of the bid. There are homeowners who turn down well-prepared contracts because these are very long (and intimidating). Because they do not understand much of the content or do not agree with parts of the contract, they opt for the contractor with the one- or two-page contract that seems less threatening. In reality, short loose-ended contracts leave the builder and the homeowner with an open-ended interpretation of materials,

content, construction methods, and builder vs. homeowner responsibilities, which can create problems. Also, a one-sided contract or a contract not fully understood is a hazard. Before signing, be sure to go over the contract with the builder in detail and have an attorney review the contract proposal.

8. *Not allowing enough room for shrinkage in the wall systems*—Never underestimate the power of shrinkage! (See question Why Is There Shrinkage in a Log Home? on page 17.)

9. *Taking on a building project beyond your experience in construction*—Without a good understanding of, or experience in, construction, a project can end in disaster, often costing much more than hiring a professional builder. Construction is much more complicated than it may appear. I understand the urge to build without practical experience, and with great embarrassment I can tell you that with our first

log home built for ourselves over twenty years ago, we made every "greenhorn" mistake that could be made. Even though I was dedicated to watching each and every Bob Vila program and reading every book I could get my hands on about construction, it simply did not compare to hands-on, practical experience learned over time. I am not saying that you cannot take on a portion of the project, but unless you have a lot of time on hand in combination with experience, your home could end up like a circus in a blender.

10. *Drinking too much coffee and overworking on job sites.* Stuff happens.

Avoiding the common pitfalls of construction and learning from others' mistakes can be direct detours away from the most common mistakes made in building.

The World According to Carpenters

We all wish to choose a contractor with the resonating bark of Tim "The Tool Man" Taylor who possesses the power to get the job done as effortlessly as Bob Vila. This is the least to hope for when hiring a contractor, since the project is only as good as the selected team leader. A good general contractor will know how to choose and manage his team well. A first-rate contractor produces a first-rate job, knowing each sub-trade's expertise and which sub-trade best fits each job.

There is nothing more satisfying than finding a builder who appreciates and understands traditional joinery methods, ensuring that your log home will be crafted with rustic charm, enthusiasm, tradition, and creativity. A good contractor's expert support will lessen the trauma of construction by paving the path from dream to reality with organization and experience.

After twenty years of building, I realize there is still so much more to learn about construction—and life! But I find myself increasingly grateful and respectful of the good craftspeople and design professionals who are paramount to the success of our projects. There are so many choices and decisions to be made on the spot during construction that can alter many areas of the project significantly, including the budget. Here are a few things to keep in mind while working with your contractor:

- The building process is a long and tedious venture. Make sure you are comfortable with your chosen contractor. If you are not comfortable up front, things only become more stressful and can spiral downhill once the "honeymoon" is over.

- Be prepared to pay fair wages. Pushing the bid too much can compromise the quality of work. The contractor and sub-trades cannot make unrealistic budgets magically work.

Adequate compensation for the contractor and sub-trades is in your best interest, as it assures the quality and level of services needed to fulfill the contract. Cost and value go hand in hand.

- If you are over budget, ask your contractor where you can cut back to help bring costs under control, although this is difficult to do in the middle of a project. Issues are best worked out up front before the work begins. Every project has unexpected costs, so don't push the budget to its limits by overextending too early in the process.

- Check references. Sometimes good contractors or sub-trades have a personality defect or one that conflicts with your own, but are talented at what they do. You must weigh what is most important to you. Also, as in any business, expect to find both those individuals who take advantage

of a situation and those who are fair and efficient. An informed consumer will have a better chance of obtaining the goal when he or she know what comprises the overall workforce and project.

• Once references have been checked and the contractor chosen, do not second-guess every decision made by him/her or attempt to micromanage the project. This does not mean you cannot ask questions or respectfully disagree with a decision made, but the contractor needs some leeway and trust to make the job run smoothly. However, if you only see a small slice of the overall project or lack experience and knowledge of the trade, it is inadvisable to override, interfere, or undermine the decision of your contractor. Also realize that there are a hundred ways to "skin a log."

- If you get to a point in the project where you know things are very wrong, take time out and possibly stop all construction to reassess the situation. This is a drastic step, but in the right situation, it may prove crucial to the success of the project.

- Contracts are one of the most easily misunderstood and neglected aspects of building a home. When construction plans are vague, the trades have an open interpretation and choice of materials or methods to be used without a set level of quality standards being determined. A written contract must be drawn up and signed before any work is started—a promise and a handshake is courting disaster, no matter how well you know the contractor. Be sure to study and fully understand all the forms before starting. (See What Do Construction Documents Consist Of? on pages 30 and 31.)

- Work with your general contractor to set budget allowances for key areas within your written contract so you can refer back to them at a later date. This budget allowance assures that you receive the equal cost of finished materials you paid for. For example, you may have in your contract a line-item budget allowance for kitchen cabinets of $9,000, but you found a style that fits your needs for only $7,000, which would leave a $2,000 credit in your contract. The most common areas for budget allowances are kitchen appliances, kitchen cabinets, doors, windows, bathroom cabinets, plumbing fixtures, and electrical fixtures.

- Don't stop the work crew to chat as the job will suffer from the constant and unnecessary interruptions. These seemingly needful interruptions can be multiplied many times over by family, friends, pets, visitors, and sightseers, and can quickly add up to lost time and money. Furthermore, an active job site can be dangerous. A small distraction can be harmful to you, your sub-trades, and those who simply should not be there.

Understanding the Design Process

Each person is special in his or her own way. We are reflections of our past, habits, interests, and experiences of life itself. The process of design is a personal journey that can be an important learning experience if you recognize and accept the reality of the compromises needed throughout the process as well as your own personal limitations.

There is no substitution for the complex, time-consuming, intensive thought process, inquiry, and research needed in the design phase. Your home's design will evolve during the planning process, where important issues will also surface. Advance planning provides improved focus and direction in expediting the overall process, thus saving cost overruns on the job site. When there are excessive on-site changes, there are often oversights made between the trades. If changes are not recorded on paper, many people involved may be overlooked or only partially informed. This does not mean that with well-thought-out designs there will be no adjustment needed, but carefully considered plans will drastically reduce the amount of wasted time and materials on-site.

Many design facilities specialize in one or more design styles. The design professional can bring different skills, experiences, interests, and values to the project. It is vitally important to find a design professional who understands this very specialized style of log building, one who will bring a high level of experience to a project to achieve a successful outcome. There is also an advantage to using a design professional independent of the log builder, as it will enable the homeowner to acquire more competitive bids from more than one log home company. Separating the design and building costs allows for a more balanced view of the overall project instead of what fits into a particular company's selling options.

Good Designs

Don't underestimate the power of good design. Detailed planning and attention to design will enhance your home and increase its value. There is also the importance of curb appeal and the flow of a home's layout. It can also bring a higher level of sophistication to the project. But the most important service a design provides is to supply meaningful information, to help make the contractor's and sub-trades' time on-site more productive. All in all, good designs will

- reflect your needs and expectations.

- assist you in securing bids from contractors and sub-trades, as well as on material supplies.

- set a higher standard of quality in construction materials and their applications.

- detail the scope of services supplied to the project.

- incorporate creative and artistic detail.

- bring clarity to making decisions about the type of log joinery to be used.

- prevent misunderstandings.

- limit disputes that can arise during construction.

What Do Construction Documents Consist Of?

There are usually three types of documents needed for construction of a log home:

The blueprints are the construction drawings, which are the largest part of your contract as well as the primary body of information supplied to the log builder, general contractor, and sub-trades. (NOTE: floor plans are not construction drawings.) Construction drawings go far beyond the realm of floor plans. The construction drawing consists of many pages (twelve or more in our plans) of dimensions, foundation plans, exterior elevations, building cross-sections, framing diagrams, typical design details, and sections that are specific to techniques used in constructing a handcrafted log structure. Construction drawings specify many details that clarify the scope of the project and help protect the homeowner's interest.

Electricity, heating, windows/doors, and interior finishes may be addressed in specifications instead of on the blueprints. Consider these two important suggestions: 1. Get your local heating/air contractor to size and locate the required heating system that works best with your climatic conditions and budget. The electrical locations may vary depending on your selected fixtures and overall electrical design, and should be decided between you and your chosen log builder. 2. Get your general contractor to prepare his or her own material list because of the differences in construction practices and local availability of materials.

The specifications are the written section of the documents with specific notations and descriptions that indicate to the builder the quality or application of the exact materials, equipment, appliances, and finish components to be included in your home. Added specifications can drastically affect the overall cost and quality of the home.

The written contract is another part of the agreement that should address who is responsible for each part of the project, outlining a clear description of responsibility for each party involved. You may not be able to anticipate all the situations that could change or be involved within a project, but some form of construction agreement should be made between the related parties for the protection of all involved. A one- or two-page written contract will not come close to covering all the issues involved in constructing a home. (Refer to the resource list for information on contracts that address the special needs of log building.) A written agreement can help avoid misunderstandings or any sense of failed expectations for either side, making hard feelings or lawsuits less likely to arise.

It is important to know and understand that cost overruns can be kept in control with quality construction documents.

Preparing for a Productive Meeting with Your Design Professional

Clear communication and realistic expectations are needed to achieve a successful project. Building in today's marketplace is a complex undertaking requiring many different products and skills. A design professional can help guide you and lessen the trauma by sorting through the mounds of information and editing it down to achieve the desired results.

Design professionals are often misunderstood and inefficiently used and/or underused in construction today at a time when they are even more necessary. There is a higher level of success in capturing the storybook look and feel of a home if a well-thought-out plan is used. If an average, under-detailed, or poor-quality plan is used, it can slow down or complicate the building process. Learning how to work effectively with your design professional can make the process enjoyable and cost-effective.

These are some of the steps you should take to clarify a custom home's design outline. Some of the items listed are also important to consider when customizing a stock plan.

Set an overall budget limit on the project.

Make a list of your needs and expectations to bring things into focus.

For a more efficient plan, make a list of all the rooms in your home, map out which rooms are used daily and for what purpose, then consolidate any of the rooms to make a more efficient plan.

Now is the time to dream up and prioritize your wish list. Then add a realistic cost beside each line item to assist you in deciding what needs to be adjusted.

Making a scrapbook of clippings with home exteriors, rooms, and details that you like will help you and your design professional focus on the look and feel you are trying to capture.

Write a list of questions to ask your design professional. Only when you outline your issues can they be addressed. Ask for an explanation of anything you don't understand; remember that a good client considers advice given by the design professional, who brings experience and specialized knowledge to a project.

Insist on obtaining a set of accurate drawings from your designer, which will give you the best interpretation of your design goals as well as a clear vision of your goals for the trades to work towards.

Making the Design Process Proceed Smoothly

- Make decisions promptly. Delaying decisions too long will only increase the possibility of change and may create conditions that upset the delicate balance between the project's time line, costs, and quality. Delays in the process can also cause the trades to lose interest and momentum, hurting the project's productivity.

- Plan for revisions. Many revisions may be required to make a design become fluid and fit your needs. It is well worth the additional costs (at this stage, the costs are minimal) to go through all the designs and adjust even the smallest of changes on paper. This can be well worth the cost of revising the plans to make sure there is a well-defined contract and clear communication between all involved.

NOTE: Typically you are allowed one round of revisions (included in the cost of the design contract) before you are charged for changes made to the plans.

- Update all agreement modifications and change orders. These contractual documents should be kept up-to-date, and in writing. Handshakes are rarely sufficient to document the agreements made even on the smallest of homes. The most simple revisions in an agreement can cause complications in the overall project and can snowball, taking on a life of their own.

- Ask questions. All questions or concerns should be addressed and resolved before construction begins. Changes made beyond this point could easily result in increased time and costs.

- Address problems or concerns. Addressing problems and concerns as they arise will help keep small issues from becoming large ones.

General Cost of Custom Designs

Good custom plans can save the cost of their initial price many times over. Hiring a design service does not necessarily mean an increase in the cost of a project unless the designer does not understand the cost of construction, has no experience with the general design formulas of log building, or is working with plans that are very vague.

It may also be worth an additional consulting fee to have a design professional who is qualified in handcrafted log building to help guide you and sort through the information specific to your needs. He or she can also give insights into money-saving alternatives that you might not have considered within your plan.

Working with a design professional does require effort on your part. You need to convey your needs clearly and set a budget limit. If you are on a tight or constricted budget, you must be honest and realistic with yourself about the home's costs.

Customizing Floor Plans to Fit Your Dreams

Working efficiently and communicating with your design professional is key for a cost-effective and focused project. You can save thousands of dollars, along with frustration and additional time spent on coordination and communication, by spending more time up front in planning. It may cost you a bit more for additional changes or tweaking of the stock plan to fit your lifestyle, but it will save you time and money later. You do not want to be working out the details while several trades are standing around on-site. Changing plans on-site can delay and affect many trades at a time and can snowball the cost of a project beyond control.

Without a doubt, stock plans are a more cost-effective solution than custom designs. But what if you find a stock plan you like but need some general design changes to fit your needs? A client recently mailed me a handwritten list of changes he wanted made to the "Weekender" stock plan

from my book, *Small Log Homes: Storybook Plans and Advice*.

"Weekender" stock-plan-customization change request:

Main Floor—

1. Living room to be widened a few feet to accommodate log stairs to a daylighted basement (using open log risers).

2. Dining nook to be cantilevered out a bit more to accommodate a built-in bench for the dining table area.

3. Master bath to be fitted with one sink and a tall linen closet.

4. What would the log home look like if I added a front-entry, covered porch?

Daylighted Basement—

1. A daylighted, usable basement with egress windows to satisfy building code requirements.

2. Bathroom to be fitted with toilet, washbasin, and shower/tub.

3. Walk-in closet to be framed within a guest bunk room.

4. Open recreation area to located at base of stairs.

5. Washer and dryer.

6. Basement to be accessed with a bulkhead door entrance.

These are all cost-effective changes that can be done quickly by using the template of a stock plan. Writing a list of the changes you would like made to a plan will give the design professional a clear idea of your wishes without the expectation of having to read each others' minds, or the risk of discussing changes but later forgetting what was agreed upon.

Here are some ideas for simple changes that can be made to stock plans.

• Change a slab basement into a walk-out basement.

• Create an in-law suite within a walk-out or daylighted basement.

• Add a garage.

- Add a timber- or log-covered porch.
- Add, move, or remove a door or window opening.
- Add or remove a fireplace.
- Add a bathroom.
- Redesign a bathroom or kitchen space.
- Change the exterior finish materials.
- Adjust the plan for handicapped accessibility.

Mirror Imaging

In some situations a log home may better suit the site with a reversed set of plans. This reversal of plans is also termed as the mirror image. Take for instance the example of Love's Cove (on page 94) shown as a reversed floor plan, or mirror image. Depending on your property location or view, you may wish to orient the house for a specific reason. For example, you may prefer the home's dining nook to capture the morning sun, or you may want to reverse the plan so you can enjoy the evening's sunset from the dining room's wraparound window.

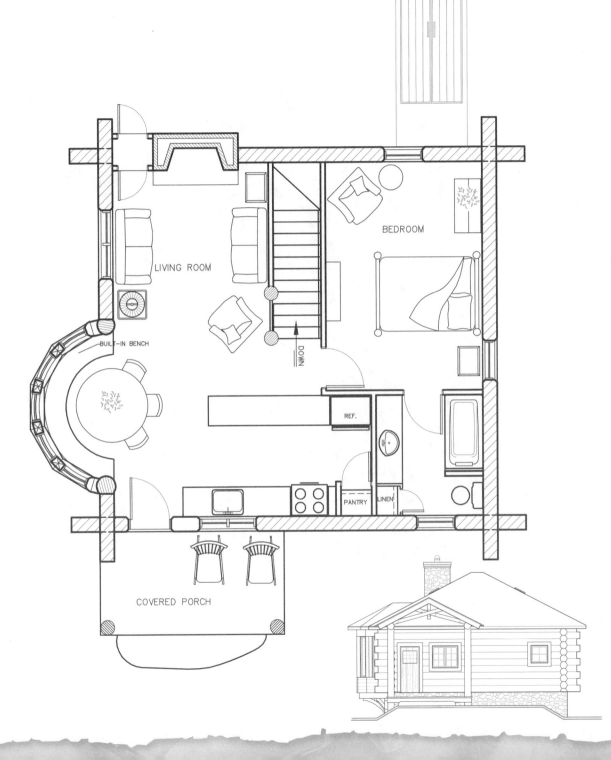

Expert Tips, Hints, and Techniques

- Understand your goals and project parameters. Take time throughout the project to regroup and reevaluate the overall project and its direction to be sure that goals and budgets are on target.

- Designing a home is full of compromises. These compromises can be turned into assets instead of liabilities by accepting your limitations and making the most of them. Many successful homes with difficult limitations were transformed into jewels when extra thought and attention were directed to their special needs.

- Each home design has its challenge; don't let it be a distraction from what is important.

- Design and decorating is not just about making things pretty, it is about thinking through every choice we make to be sure it is something we would use well.

- Read, read, and read some more. If something is helpful and informative, read it again to absorb more each time. Creating a good base of information is vital to making educated decisions. Be well informed so that specific questions will address your needs. Knowledge is empowering and enables confidence in choices made during the process of building.

- Go over the blueprints to understand the content of the design.

- Save one set of blueprints to highlight with areas to ask questions, then choose one color to highlight those for the log builder, another color for the general contractor, and a third color for the design professional.

- In one or two sittings with the design professional or contractor, compile a written list of questions and notes that organizes a focused discussion. When phone calls or meetings are unplanned and dragged out into many short occurrences over a long period of time, it will drain the attention of the design professional or contractor.

Developing Character

- Sit or camp on the property many times to absorb the surroundings. Take into consideration that houses do not need to line up straight with the road, tree lines, fences, etc. A good design will take advantage of the property's grades, surrounding landscape, daylight patterns, and views.

- A fireplace can take the chill off even the coldest of winter nights. There is something romantic about a log home with the warmth of a fireplace, but if the budget does not allow for a fireplace, direct all efforts and attention to other areas of the home to give it punch. Some of the most charming log homes do not have fireplaces, vaulted ceilings, or large footprints.

- Porches can be designed as extensions of the home's living and dining areas. They can be relaxing places to unwind after a long day at work or a great place for a nap in the gentle summer breeze.

- Generous roof overhangs and exposed rafters make the roof appear to embrace a home as well as add protection for the walls and windows. The overhangs themselves are forms of ornamentation and can make even the simplest home appear luxurious and well grounded.

- The power of color can be incorporated into a home to add a subtle spark or an electrifying mix or vibrancy, making even a boring space come to life.

- Take some added time to bring character into an entrance that invites all who enter, thus providing great curb appeal for the home.

- Look over and assess each room individually, as the challenge in good design is to give each room personality and develop efficient use of each and every space.

- Varying the ceiling heights can create powerful visual interest and drama in a home.

- Incorporate nature and select materials for their indigenous qualities to help blend the home into its surroundings.

- Try using old cast-iron radiators for heat instead of radiant floor tubing. Old radiators are so easy to refurbish, retrofit, and maintain, and they radiate an even, comfortable heat while recycling a piece of history.

Bare Necessities

- It is not about how large or expensive a log home is that makes a house a home, but how inviting and comfortable the space feels. Often, the dream of a simple cabin in the woods can be overtaken by the complexities in life. Simplicity in itself can be spectacular. There is a sense of freedom in living a more simple life in balance with nature.

- If a project is out of a realistic budget range, scale down and rethink it through. A lot of space isn't necessary to live in comfort.

- For a custom design it may often take a year or more of research, planning, and designing prior to starting construction. Stock plans can help reduce the average time frame spent developing a design concept by 60 to 90 percent.

- Create a multipurpose floor plan with design flexibility by planning spaces that can be used for more then one activity to maximize space, such as using the office as a guest room; incorporating a sunroom into a dining room or office area; doubling up the laundry with a bathroom or closet; or incorporating the formal living room, dining room, and family room into one space. When the usefulness and purpose of each space is planned and considered, then a home is used more efficiently.

Budget Limitations

Budget constraints can evolve into creative solutions, so don't give up the dream just because of a limited budget. Downsizing the list of wants and reducing material items will allow a more direct focus on living. Wasted space costs money. Here are just a few money-saving ideas that were successfully generated with budget limitations.

- Hand-built kitchen shelving with cloth fronts covering the base shelves instead of the standard kitchen cabinets and door fronts is a design alternative that is cost-effective while creating a romantic look with old-fashioned charm.

- Pantries can house three times or more dry goods and equipment than regular kitchen cabinets. Site-built pantries to house dry goods allows for minimal need of store-bought cabinetry.

- Kitchen cupboards made of yard-sale finds and flea-market funk create a casual old-time look that can be added to over a period of time.

- Build bare-minimum kitchen-cabinet frames of twig saplings, either with bark or hand-peeled. Shelves can be created by using planking or plywood.

- Build an outhouse instead of an extra bathroom. Beautifully built privies can become great conversation pieces and accommodate the overflow of visitors.

- Painted plywood floors can be creatively finished for a sense of whimsy and fun, such as a hopscotch design on the bedroom floor or a roadway painted in the recreation room or the kids' bedrooms. Try painting plywood with more subtle tones to make the floors "disappear." Once furnishings are in place, plywood floors left in their raw state are not even noticeable.

- Add a bay window instead of a room for extra seating, a mini-sunroom for fresh herbs, or a hideaway nook for reading a favorite book.

- Spend additional time on closet planning for the most effective use of space. Closets are often overlooked and under-planned. A well-designed closet can easily add three times the storage space within the same footprint.

- Sew fabric panels instead of putting in doors to the pantry, living room, or bedroom. This can promote good ventilation while still providing privacy to a space.

Building for the Future

Present and future housing is often predicated on design concepts that are cold and sterile—using chrome, large expanses of glass, plastics, and hard surfaces, and vast empty spaces. I often wonder if technological building advancements and these cold materials will bring happiness to the homeowner. I find it more accurate to rely on tried-and-true classic construction forms that utilize natural materials. When these basic natural materials are incorporated into the structure, the finished home will radiate warmth, character, and personality. It is hard to outdo nature.

To build for the future should be to create a home where simplicity is valued more than overindulgence of material possessions. Many homeowners have become slaves to so many modern-day conveniences, trinkets, and endless possessions. Perhaps we do not need to reinvent the home, but reinvent ourselves. With sensitivity to surroundings and attention to priorities, we can build with a commitment to make a difference and with a passion to get down to the basics of what is really needed—where less is more.

Many homes built today often contain a lot of wasted or poorly planned space. There is great satisfaction in constructing a smaller, more thoughtfully built home with natural materials and renewable resources that are not highly processed. A well-crafted structure will age with grace and retain its classic beauty for future generations to enjoy. These beautifully built structures transcend time with grace and elegance and are always in style, radiating warmth and acquiring a subtle patina as time passes by.

It may be hard to find builders and design professionals who are willing to make the change to more environmentally protective structures, but they are out there! However, if someone who understands this cannot be found, research the proper materials (or add to your specification lists) that are needed in your home and make them part of the construction contract. As a consumer, insist on taking the extra time, effort, and cost to research ways to protect the environment; promoting this worthy concept can, and will, make a difference.

The Designer Series Stock Plans

These construction drawings provide the information necessary to efficiently construct a log home, with illustrations and specifications that show the special connections needed to build a handcrafted log home. All plans are easily translated into a milled or manufactured log home building style, as well as any 2 x 6 conventional-style layout with log elements (i.e., conventional 2 x 6 constructed walls complemented with log trusses, log stairs, log railings, and covered porches with log roof systems). At times, the working drawings may vary from the book's conceptual drawings, but these variances are minimal.

Each log home has undergone numerous studies of interior-space utilization to maximize every square foot of each room by analyzing traffic patterns, locating doors and windows, and detailing specification and illustrations of junction for both conventional 2 x 6 construction and log work.

Included in most stock plans

- Foundation plans (be sure to ask for foundation type when ordering).

- Floor plans, including the position and dimensions of walls, windows, doors, etc.

- Log wall as well as conventional wall sections.

- All exterior elevations, including front, side, and rear.

- General notes recommending specifications for quality standards in the handcrafted trade.

- Illustrations to clarify portions of cross sections or design details

- Illustrated shrinkage details and unusual connection ideas that relate to the sub-trades and log builder.

- Suggested materials appropriate for the exterior's finish detail.

Not included in all stock plans

- Material quantity lists (to be obtained by your chosen contractor or from your local building supplier, due to regional material availability and individual contractor preferences of building applications).

- Heating, plumbing, and electrical plan layout (due to regional code variation or climate requirements).

Reverse plans

In some situations a log home may better suit the site with a reverse set of plans. The plan's lettering and dimensions will not appear backwards on the reverse set with design imaging equipment technologies.

Building Codes and Verification

Plans are designed to meet Standard Building Code, but because of varying interpretations and the fact that codes and ordinances continually change and differ from region to region, we cannot warrant compliance with any of the specific building codes and ordinances. A general contractor should review the plans to verify his use and methods of building practices and to ensure that they comply with all applicable codes and requirements. The contractor should also verify all dimensions and square-foot calculations, while taking into consideration any modifications or additions that may be made in the plans.

Whistling Crow

Main Floors: 1,437 square feet • Basement: 952 square feet (with garage)

This three-bedroom log cabin classic is cost-effective to construct. The main floor has an open living room, dining room, and U-shaped kitchen area. The home's core is warmed by a fireplace, which is wrapped by stairs that wind up and behind the chimney's stack. One of the three bedrooms is located on the main floor with his-and-her closets and a bathroom nearby.

The upstairs bedrooms are packed full of closets and knee-wall storage space. The log roof system's structural elements are exposed for all to enjoy.

The backdoor covering stoop enters into a mudroom with a washer and dryer and additional closet space. There is also a full walkout basement with garage and a bonus room for the kids' recreation, a media room, or workshop.

Its textured exterior gables are created by randomly placed cedar shingles that give this classic cabin its rustic charm, reflecting the character of a secluded camp while incorporating modern-day conveniences.

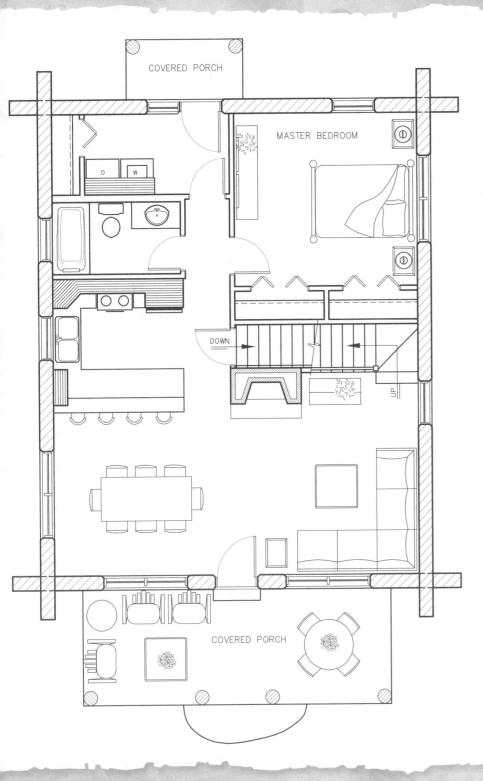

COVERED PORCH

MASTER BEDROOM

D   W

DOWN

UP

COVERED PORCH

51

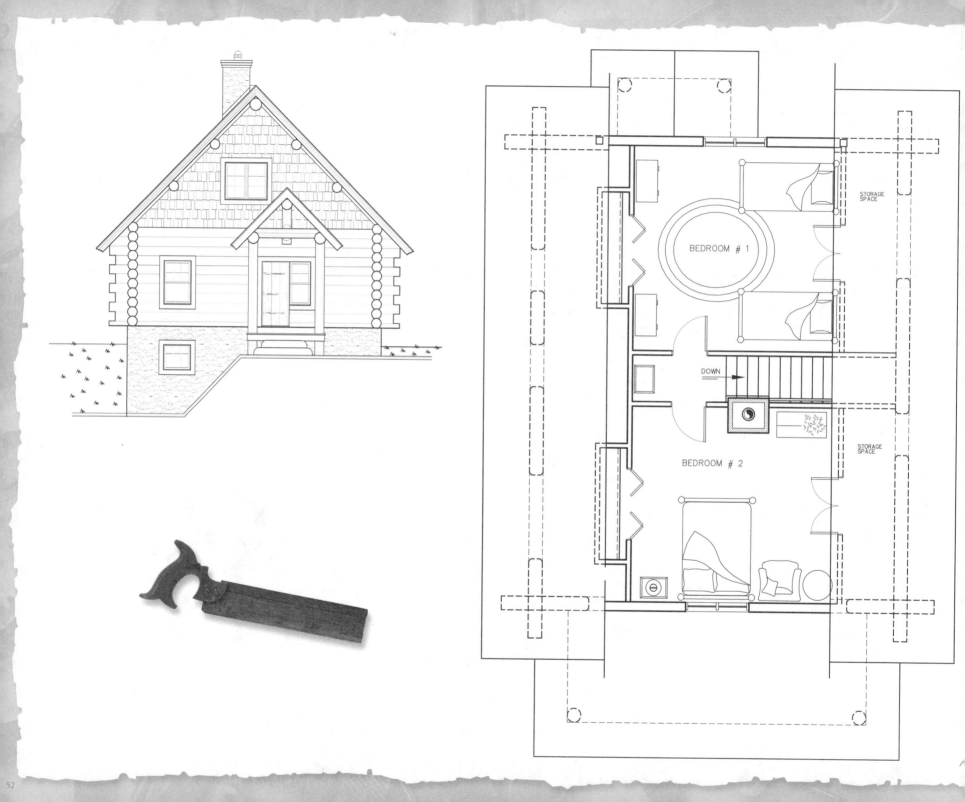

BEDROOM # 1

STORAGE SPACE

DOWN

STORAGE SPACE

BEDROOM # 2

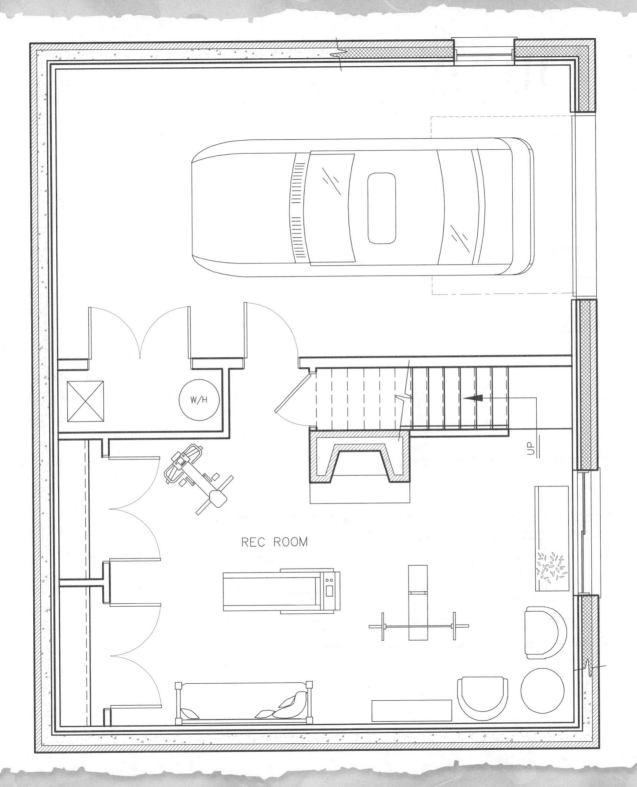

REC ROOM

W/H

UP

Camp Firefly

Main Floors: 1,430 square feet • Basement: 830 square feet (walkout)

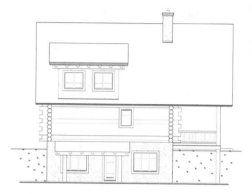

This small storybook cabin creates a lot of living in such a small footprint! Efficient use of space, attention to detail, carved-out nooks, and built-in charm add to this not-so-average log home. This fairytale log cabin was carefully planned by creating wrap-around covered porches, a bump-out bed that feels like a playhouse among the treetops, and an outdoor fireplace in which to roast marshmallows or by which to tell a good story.

The main floor of the home enters into a very large and spacious living room with the warm glow of a fireplace hearth. The French doors swing out onto a covered porch that never seems to end. The porch expands the home's square footage to include outdoor

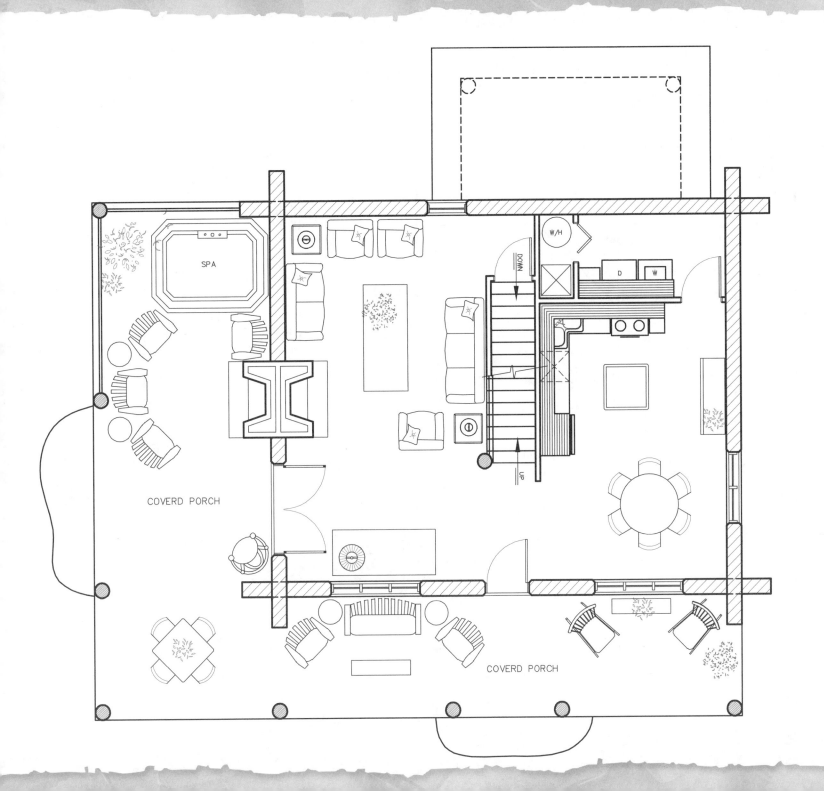

SPA

COVERD PORCH

W/H

D   W

DOWN

UP

COVERD PORCH

55

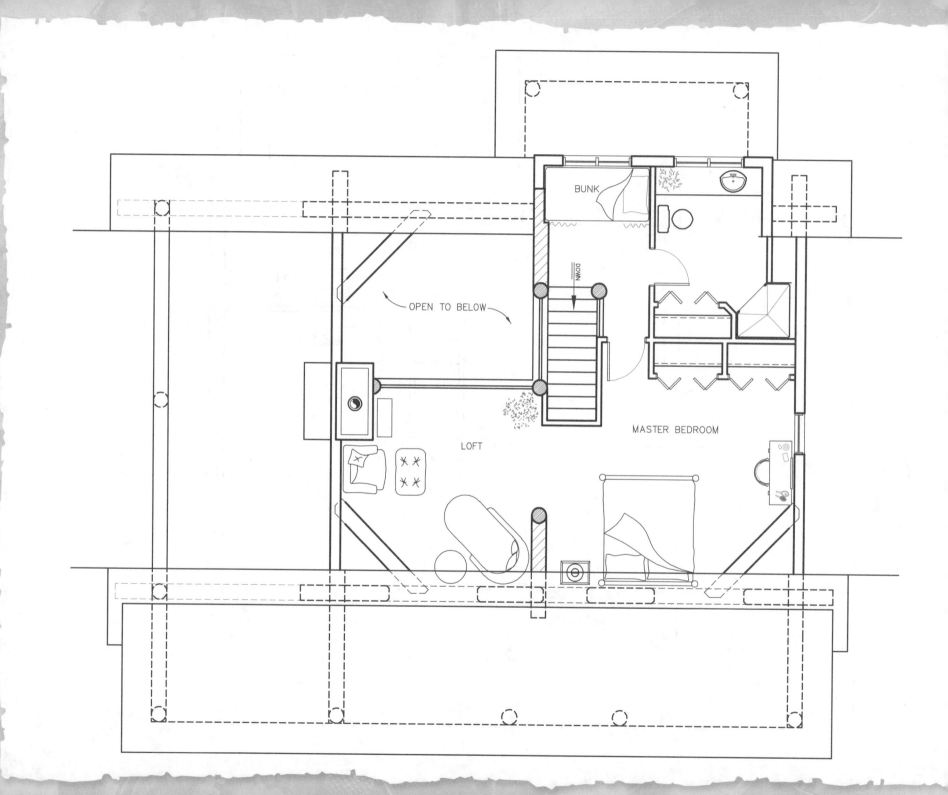

BUNK

OPEN TO BELOW

DOWN

MASTER BEDROOM

LOFT

fun. The country kitchen has ample room with a large butler's pantry and the convenience of a full-sized washer, dryer, and a lot of shelving.

The upstairs loft is a wonderful retreat with a bump-out bathroom and great detailing within the log-rafter roof system. The bedroom suite has a cozy reading nook that perches high above the living room. The basement's in-law suite could also be used as the kids' bunkroom or media room. The suite is versatile enough for many incarnations. The open floor plan has a great kitchenette. The bathroom has its own washer/dryer for self-sufficiency. The walkout basement has a private covered porch made of log rafters for even more outdoor fun.

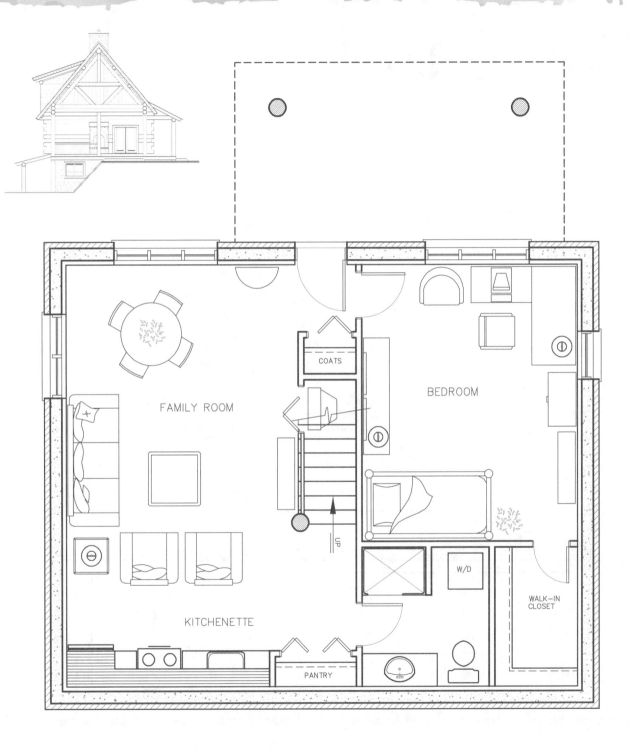

FAMILY ROOM

BEDROOM

COATS

KITCHENETTE

UP

W/D

WALK-IN
CLOSET

PANTRY

Star Gazer

Main Floors: 1,525 square feet • Basement: 950 square feet (daylight)

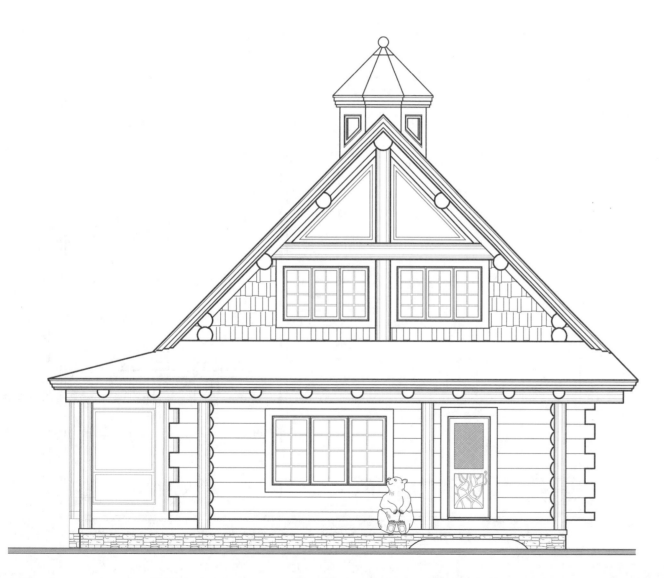

This log home creates a dramatic look from any angle. It is the essence of a fairytale log cabin with cottage charm. Even though the home has a small footprint, it makes good use of every inch of space, incorporating three bedrooms and two full bathrooms into its plan.

The wraparound porch is a classic American tradition that suits this home. The main floor great room has a well-proportioned living space wrapped in log walls. The U-shaped kitchen has an effective work triangle. The counter's wide ledge is designed for a breakfast bar. The dining-area sunroom, made of full-log post-and-beam–style construction, will chase away the winter blues with three sides of the room wrapped in large panes of glass.

The upstairs has a romantic master loft that includes a walk-in closet and wonderful spa-style bathroom. The convenience of a separate shower and a soaking- or jetted-tub is a great combination of luxury and relaxation.

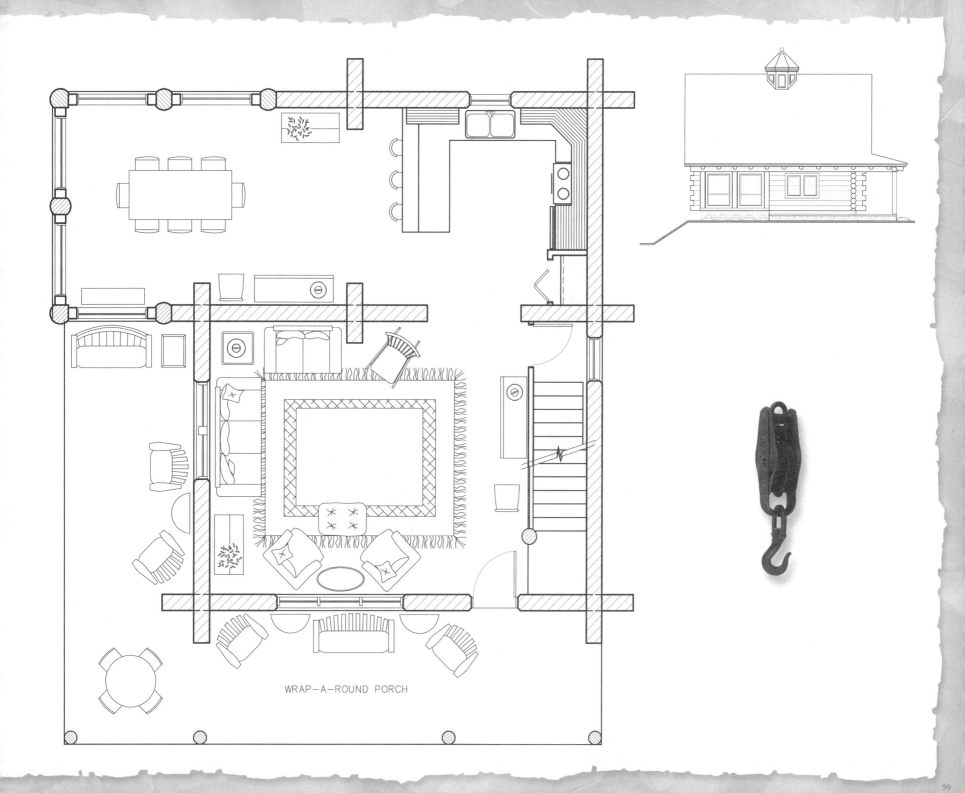

WRAP-A-ROUND PORCH

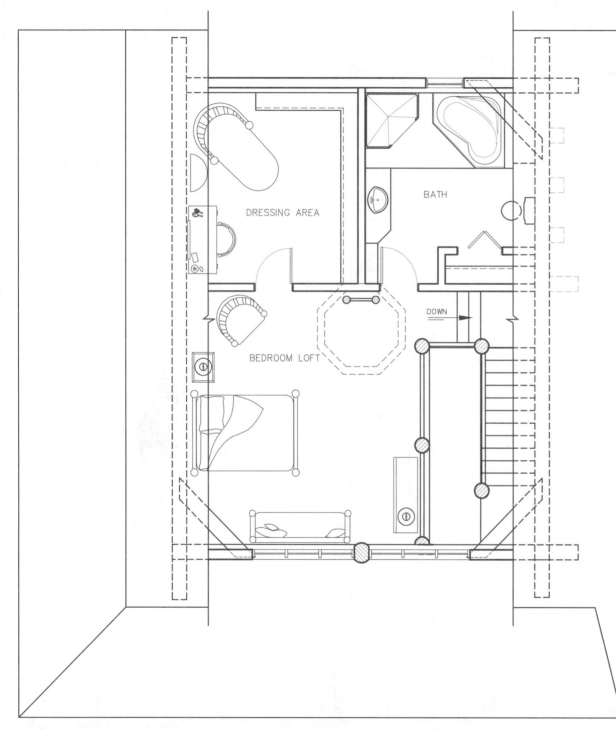

DRESSING AREA

BATH

BEDROOM LOFT

DOWN

This is a master retreat that will provide a bit of vacation without leaving home.

The daylighted basement is the perfect place for the kids' private area, with plenty of design flexibility and ample closets for all those things collected in life. The large family room does well as a media and/or game room. The secluded, one-floor suite provides the kids with a sense of independence by allowing them their very own space.

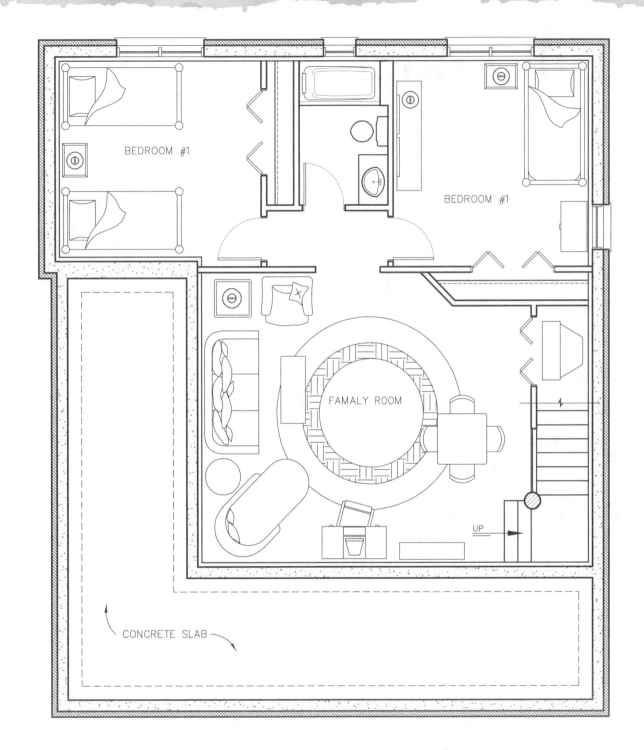

BEDROOM #1

BEDROOM #1

FAMALY ROOM

UP

CONCRETE SLAB

Birch Hill Lodge

Main Floors: 1,500 square feet • Basement: 980 square feet (walkout)

Tucked into the hillside, the three-sided wraparound porch becomes an integral part of the structure's overall design. The asymmetrical design emphasizes a connection with nature. Windows are placed strategically to capture the sweeping views: just sit back from anywhere in this log home and enjoy a year's worth of changing seasons.

The wraparound kitchen makes efficient use of space with plenty of cabinets, pantry space, and countertops. A great little breakfast bar allows guests to entertain you while you prepare that night's fare of food and fun.

The first-floor bedroom could be used as a den/guestroom or a more formal dining area. The mudroom entry has convenient access to a three-quarter bath. The home is designed to fit into the handcrafted style of the centuries-old art form of meticulously scribe-fitted logs. Don't let the simplicity and clean lines of this log structure fool you. Years of knowledge in handcrafted log work are needed to create this illusion of simplicity.

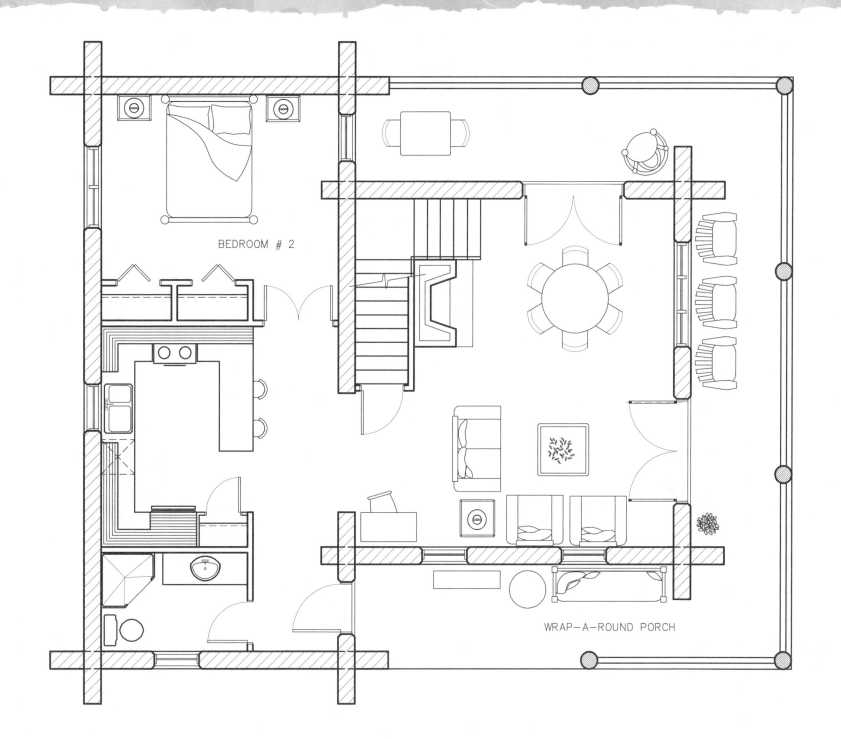

BEDROOM # 2

WRAP-A-ROUND PORCH

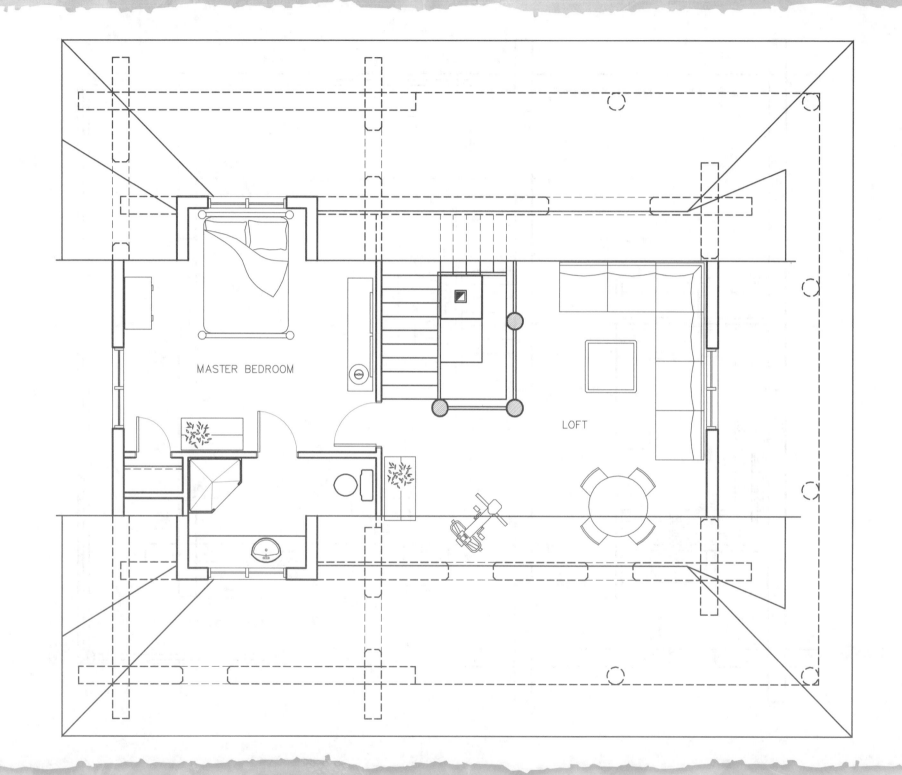

MASTER BEDROOM

LOFT

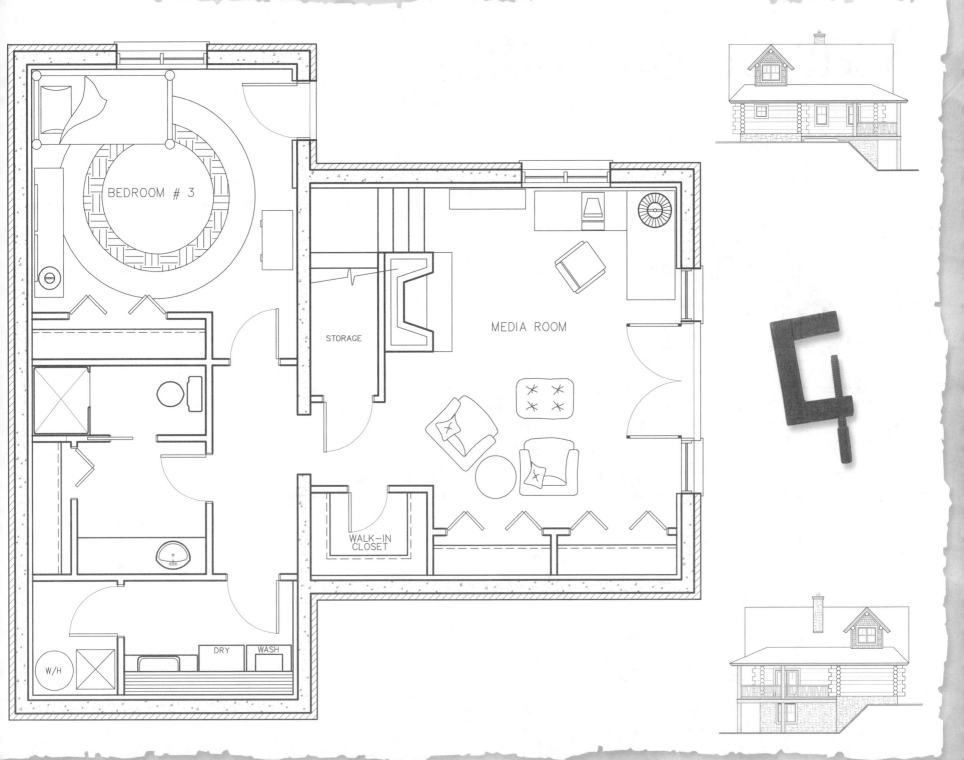

BEDROOM # 3

STORAGE

MEDIA ROOM

WALK-IN CLOSET

DRY

WASH

W/H

Bear Creek Lodge

Main Floors: 2,255 square feet • Basement: 1,354 square feet (walkout)

This log home has been a very popular design. Its gracious wraparound porch allows for many square feet of additional outdoor living. The covered porch is a great American tradition that adds a touch of romance with its porch swings, tea tables, rocking chairs, and slat-backed benches. Today's amenities such as hot tubs and outdoor fireplaces have added a new spin to the outdoor porch. The covered porch is a classic that will never go out of style.

This log home has an elegant entry opening into a large great room that focuses on an oversized circular log staircase. There is a living room bump-out that houses a large grouping of furnishings for an inviting conversation. The great room incorporates a dining room bay that gives the feel of a miniature conservatory, allowing a flood of light to warm the room. The home's circular stairs sweep up to a loft perched above the great room. It is a multifunctional space that can be used as a den, an office, or a bunk loft.

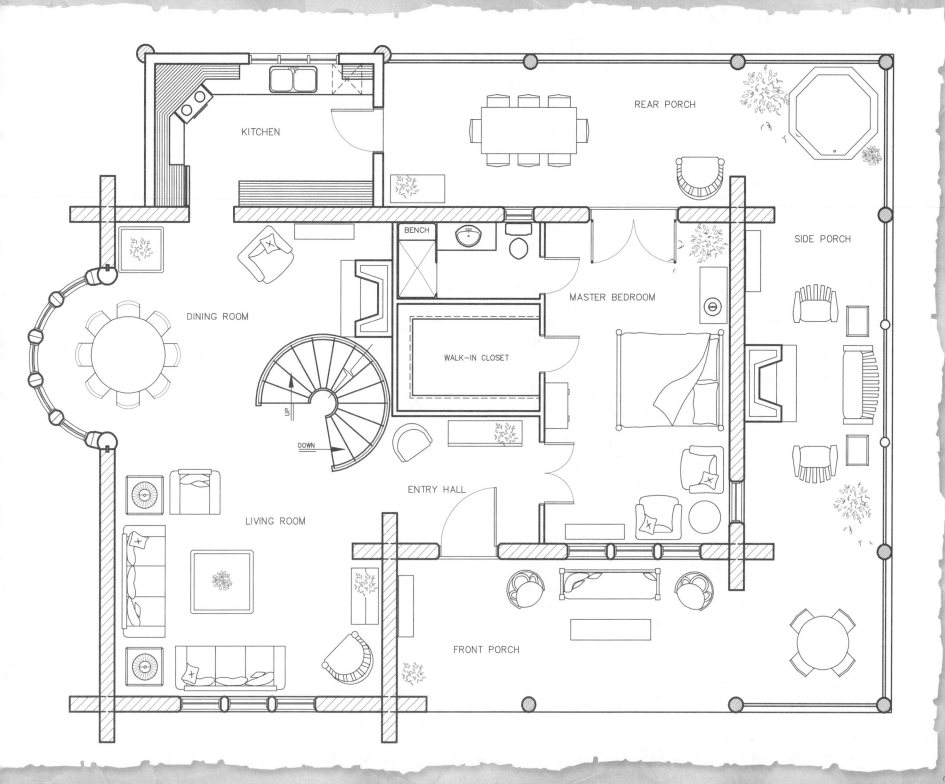

KITCHEN

REAR PORCH

SIDE PORCH

BENCH

MASTER BEDROOM

DINING ROOM

WALK-IN CLOSET

UP

DOWN

ENTRY HALL

LIVING ROOM

FRONT PORCH

67

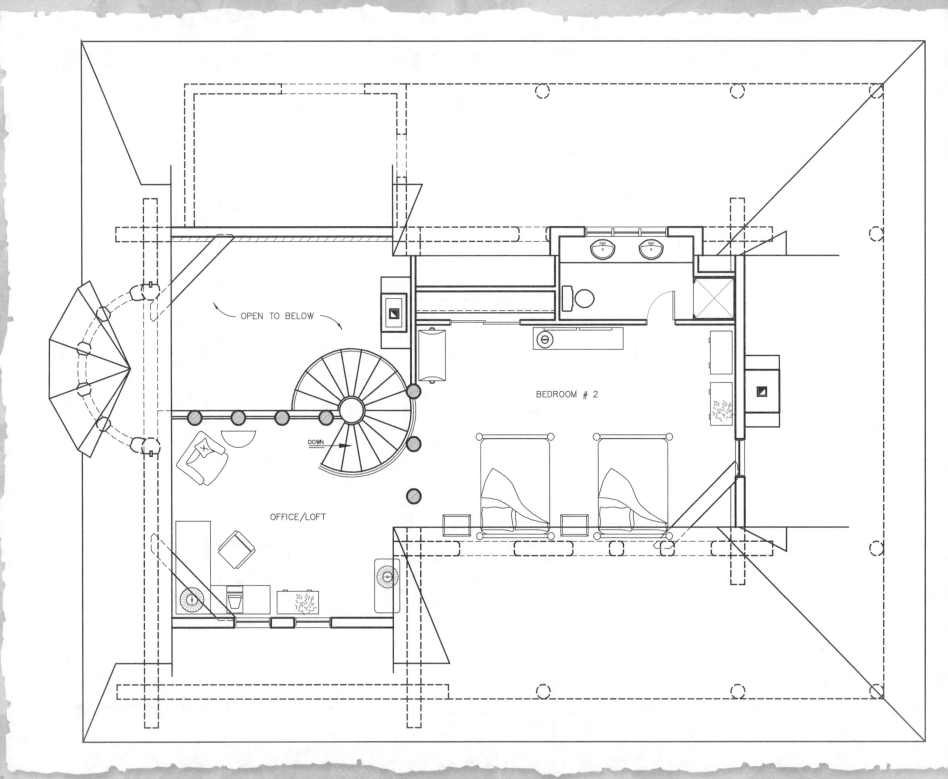

OPEN TO BELOW

BEDROOM # 2

DOWN

OFFICE/LOFT

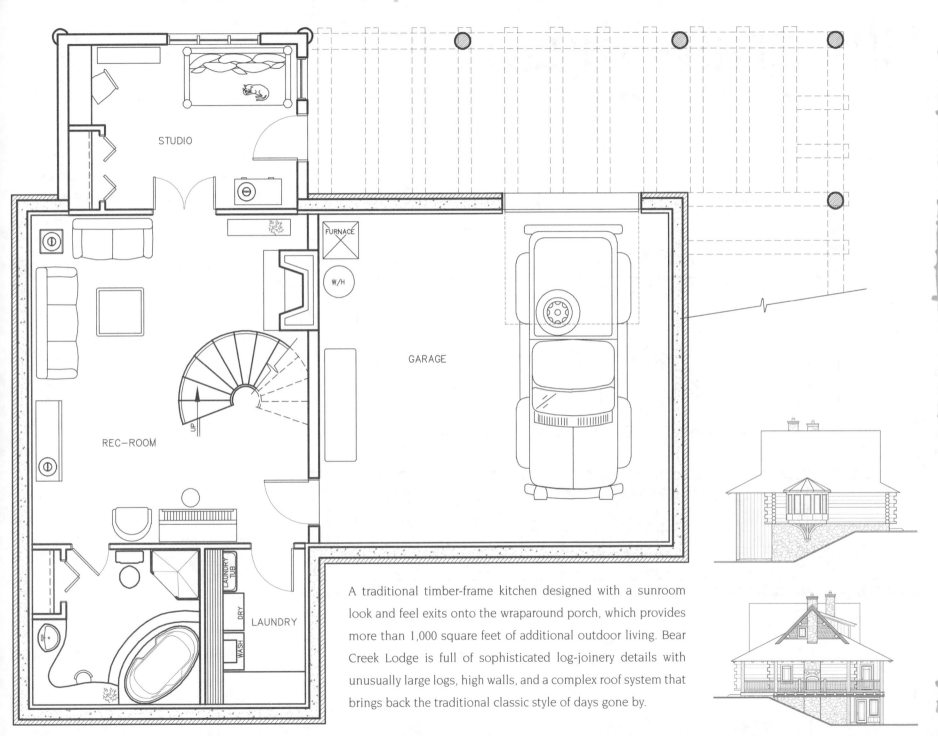

STUDIO

FURNACE

W/H

GARAGE

REC—ROOM

UP

LAUNDRY TUB

DRY

WASH

LAUNDRY

A traditional timber-frame kitchen designed with a sunroom look and feel exits onto the wraparound porch, which provides more than 1,000 square feet of additional outdoor living. Bear Creek Lodge is full of sophisticated log-joinery details with unusually large logs, high walls, and a complex roof system that brings back the traditional classic style of days gone by.

Bluegrass Ridge

Main Floors: 2,000 square feet • Basement: 1,280 square feet (with garage)

This one-and-a-half-story log shell is an efficient layout that makes the most of a handcrafted, four-corner structure. The staircase wanders up and around the masonry fireplace, which has a pizza oven built into its side. The home has plenty of pantry and closet space to house family mementos. The entryway hides kitchen clutter from arriving guests. The first-floor ceilings are a luxurious ten feet high. The four-sided covered porch provides an additional 1,200 square feet of living space.

The upstairs loft has a spacious master bedroom suite that vaults up fifteen feet. The stairs landing loft is shown as a library or office space, but it could function in many different ways. The loft overlooks the great room.

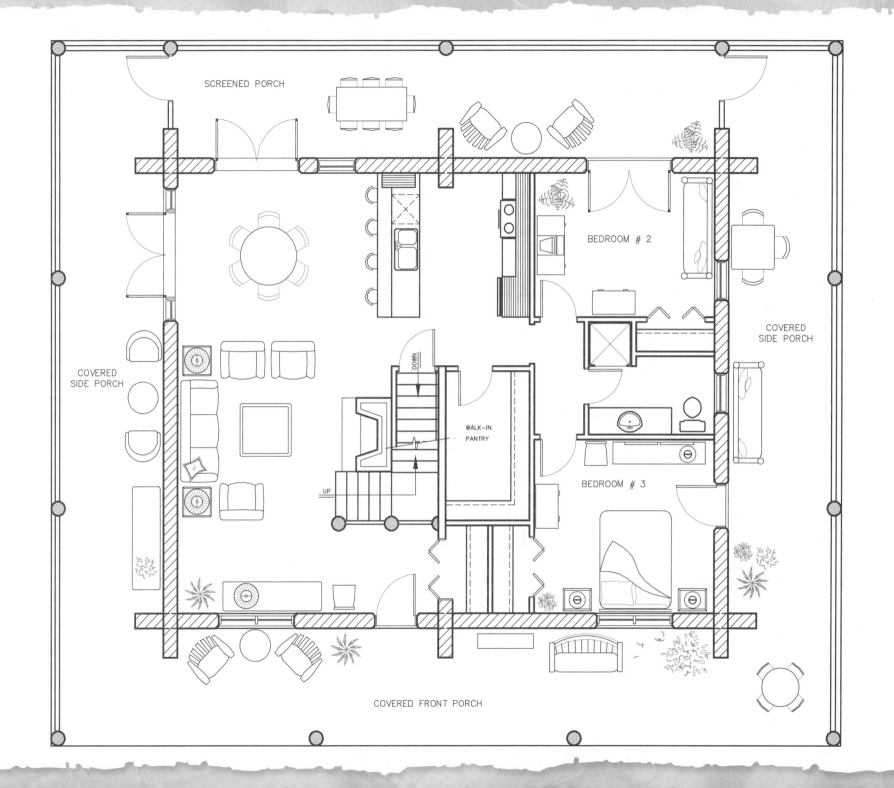

SCREENED PORCH

COVERED
SIDE PORCH

BEDROOM # 2

COVERED
SIDE PORCH

DOWN

WALK-IN
PANTRY

UP

BEDROOM # 3

COVERED FRONT PORCH

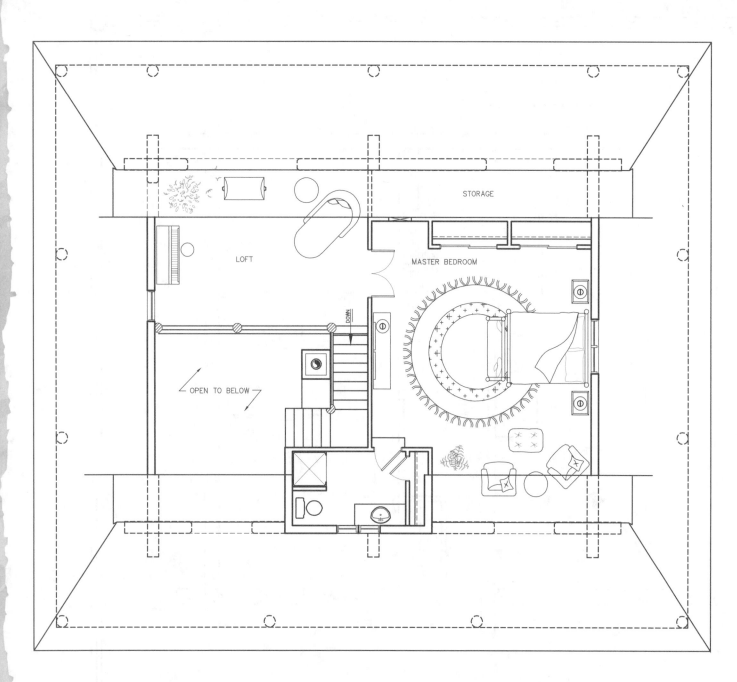

STORAGE

LOFT

MASTER BEDROOM

DOWN

OPEN TO BELOW

The basement is designed to accommodate a garage. The laundry room
and garage are accessible to both the
main house and the in-law suite. The
in-law suite has an open floor plan
that maximizes its limited space. The
bedroom has a walk-in closet and a
bathroom that makes the most of its
square footage.

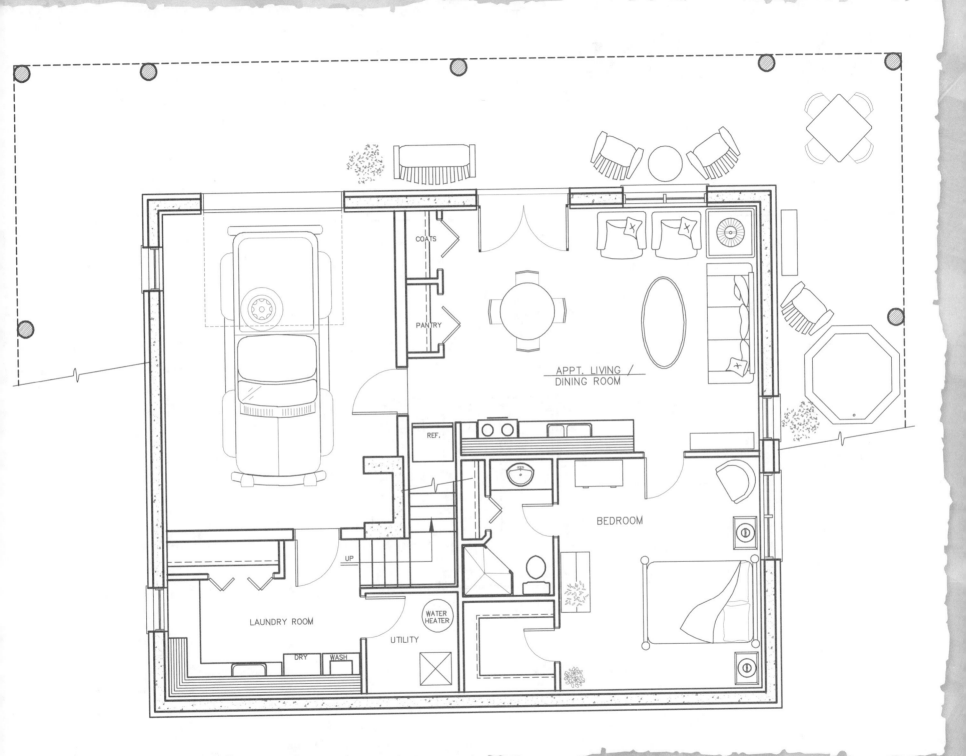

COATS

PANTRY

APPT. LIVING /
DINING ROOM

REF.

BEDROOM

UP

WATER
HEATER

LAUNDRY ROOM

UTILITY

DRY   WASH

Lime Hollow

Main Floors: 2,435 square feet • Basement: 1,730 square feet (with garage)

This large log home has five bedrooms and four bathrooms. The design uses many intersecting log walls to create individual rooms. One of the home's three covered porches opens into the home's entry hall. A conveniently located first-floor study has its own private bathroom. The country kitchen rambles on with plenty of dining room area and a U-shaped kitchen layout; an extended counter provides extra space for a breakfast bar. There is a set of gracefully designed, arched-top patterned French doors that open onto a covered balcony. The kitchen's log walls have a soft archway cut into the log header beam that spills into the great room. The living room's focal point is the oversized fireplace, with a set of stairs that curls around the fireplace hearth. The upstairs loft has two more private bedroom wings with a

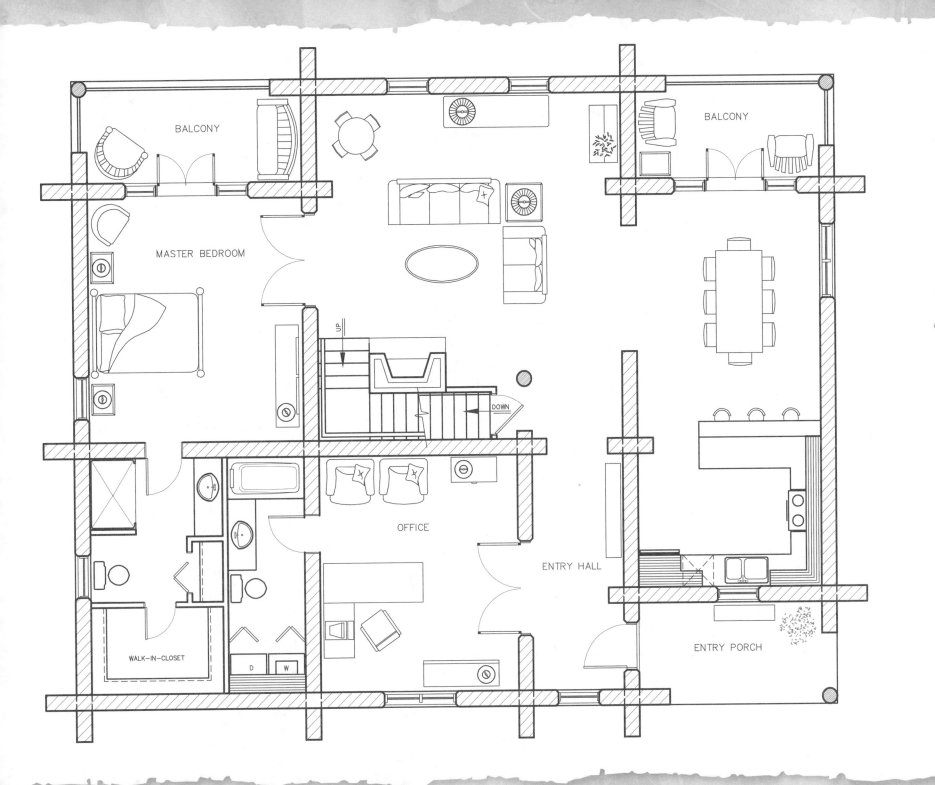

BALCONY

BALCONY

MASTER BEDROOM

OFFICE

ENTRY HALL

ENTRY PORCH

WALK-IN-CLOSET

UP

DOWN

D W

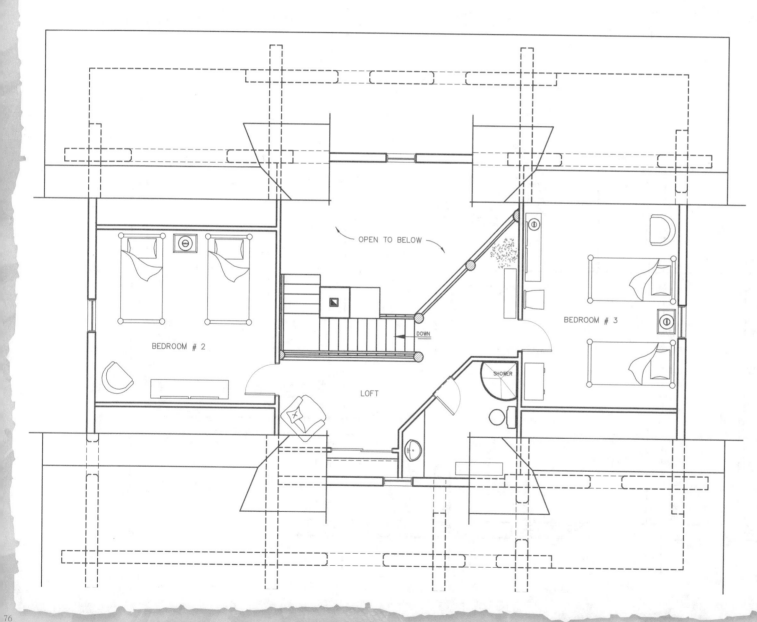

OPEN TO BELOW

BEDROOM # 2

DOWN

LOFT

SHOWER

BEDROOM # 3

shared bathroom located in the galley bridge that overlooks the living area below.

The first-floor master bedroom is a special retreat in which all four walls are wrapped in logs. A bathroom and walk-in closet are carefully tucked into the master suite. The bedroom's outdoor balcony is perfect for morning tea or as an afternoon hideaway to read the weekend paper.

The full-sized basement has a large recreation room that includes the warmth of a fireplace. There are two more bedrooms and a shared bath, as well as a general-purpose room with a walk-in closet. This large area could easily be transformed into a kitchen/dining room for an in-law suite. The garage is incorporated into the home's walkout basement, with a utility room located in the back.

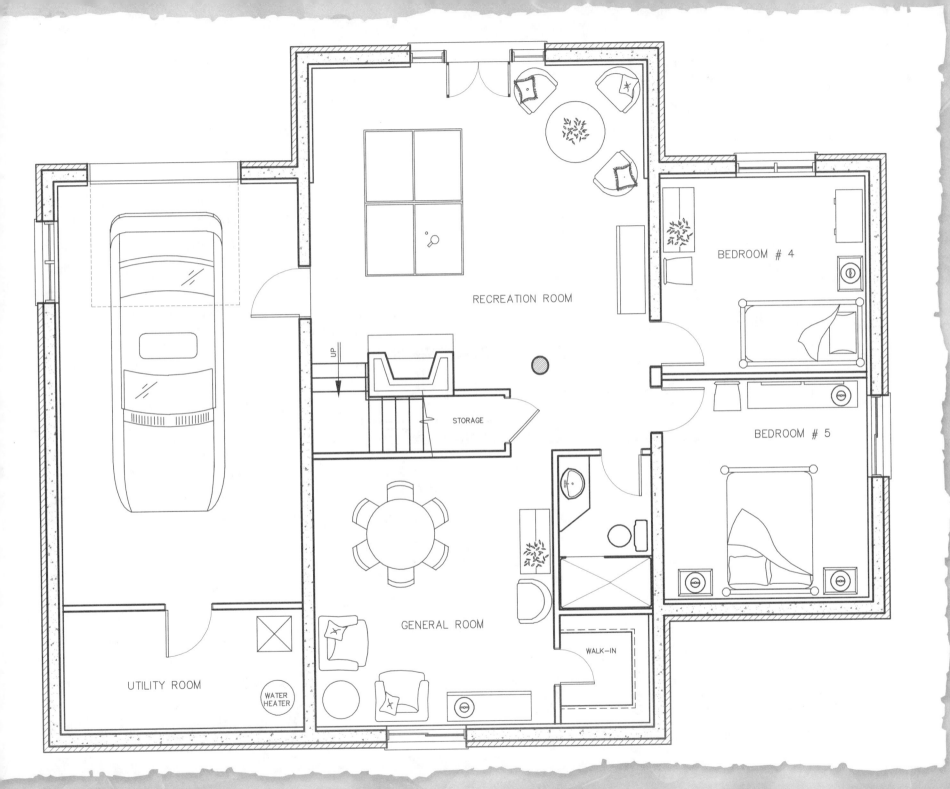

RECREATION ROOM

BEDROOM # 4

BEDROOM # 5

UP

STORAGE

GENERAL ROOM

WALK-IN

UTILITY ROOM

WATER
HEATER

Deer Valley

Main Floor: 1,944 square feet

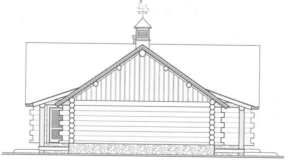

This T-shaped log home has three bedrooms and two bathrooms—all designed for optimum one-floor living. The porches and patio provide a wonderful mix of outdoor living space, allowing many cozy spots for relaxing—dining, hot tubbing, sitting on porch swings, and more.

The great room has several massive log-web trusses and purlins. The purlins sit on top of the trusses, spanning the full length of the public space. Large plates of glass fill the gable-end trusses, allowing the low winter sun to flood the home with light. There is the added warmth of an old-fashioned woodstove and a large corner pantry for all those necessary winter provisions.

There are many interesting features incorporated into this log home, such as a mudroom entry with a bench, plenty of storage, and a washer and dryer; a master bedroom shower bench; and many closets throughout. The cost-saving design of a conventional roof system is built over the bedroom wing. There are large log floor joists overhead, mortised into the bedroom walls to give the ceilings the illusion of a full upstairs.

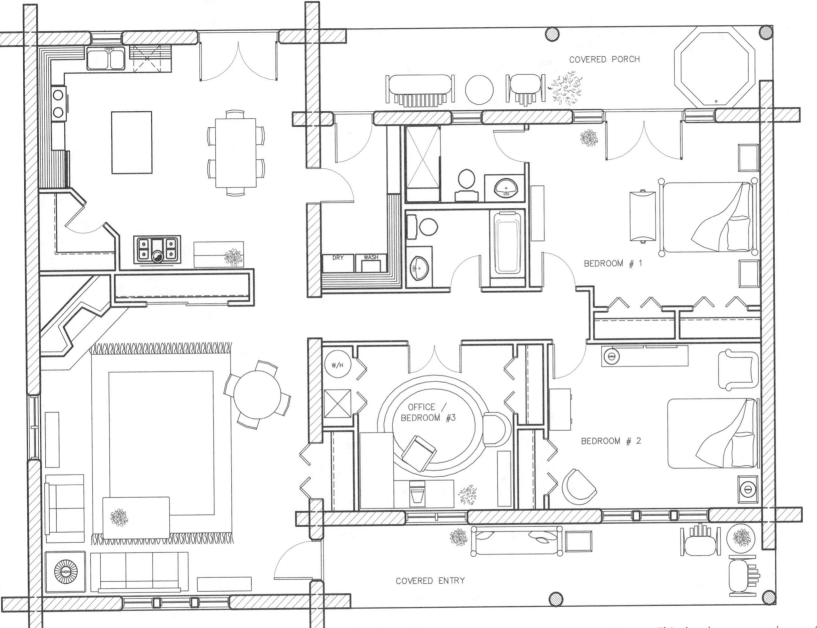

COVERED PORCH

DRY WASH

BEDROOM # 1

OFFICE / BEDROOM #3

BEDROOM # 2

W/H

COVERED ENTRY

This log home was chosen for its clean and simple lines. It is a log home classic with an earthy feel, filled with the natural power and beauty of log home living.

Sweet Grass

Main Floors: 2,178 square feet • Basement: 1,280 square feet (walkout)

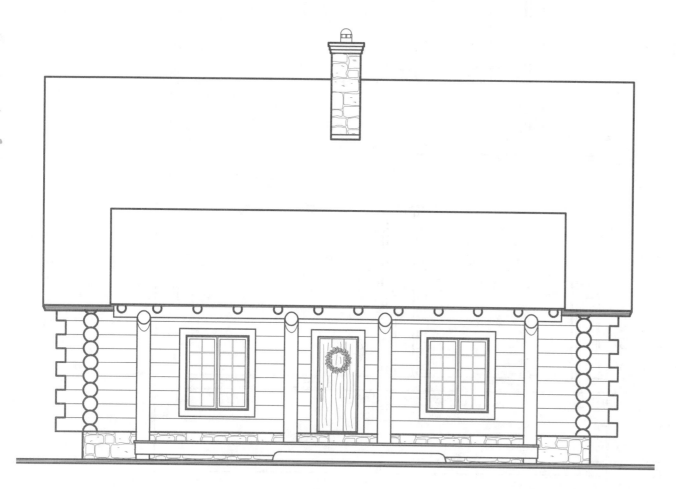

This house is classic simplicity with two homes in one. The bonus of a walkout basement expands the living space to accommodate a full-sized, self-contained in-law or caretaker's apartment. This suite is large, airy, filled with light, and does not feel at all like a basement. This full basement is an economical use of space, because it doubles the living area without adding more foundation, structural wall systems, and additional roof systems. This home allows for a total of 3,458 feet of living space, all within a conservative footprint, creating the look and feel of a storybook log home that is far larger than it appears.

The main floor is spacious with a comfortable flow of space and classic features. The many porches are an amenity that enhances the appeal of the home. The center of attention within the house is a large fireplace and wraparound, heated stone bench. The kitchen has a block island that invites good friends and good food into an area where one never feels trapped.

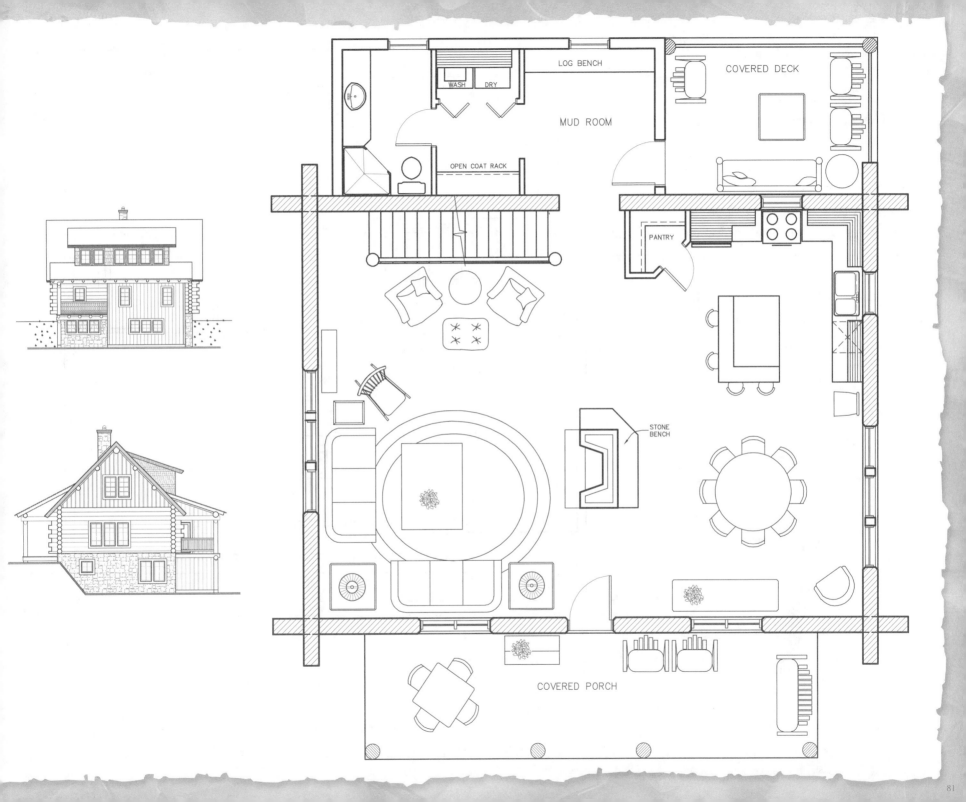

LOG BENCH

WASH DRY

MUD ROOM

COVERED DECK

OPEN COAT RACK

PANTRY

STONE
BENCH

COVERED PORCH

81

The mudroom, laundry, and bathroom at the back of the house are conventionally built with 2 x 6 walls that create a beautiful contrast of log rafters within the shed roof system. There is a storage bench built into the mudroom, with plenty of coat racks and additional shelving space above the washer and dryer. A large balcony located off the mudroom is a cozy sitting area, perfect for enjoying morning tea or absorbing the great outdoors. The upstairs has a natural sunlit landing, with massive log columns and dramatic wall angles that add great architectural interest. There are two large bedrooms with an abundance of closets. The structural elements of the log roof system are exposed for all to enjoy.

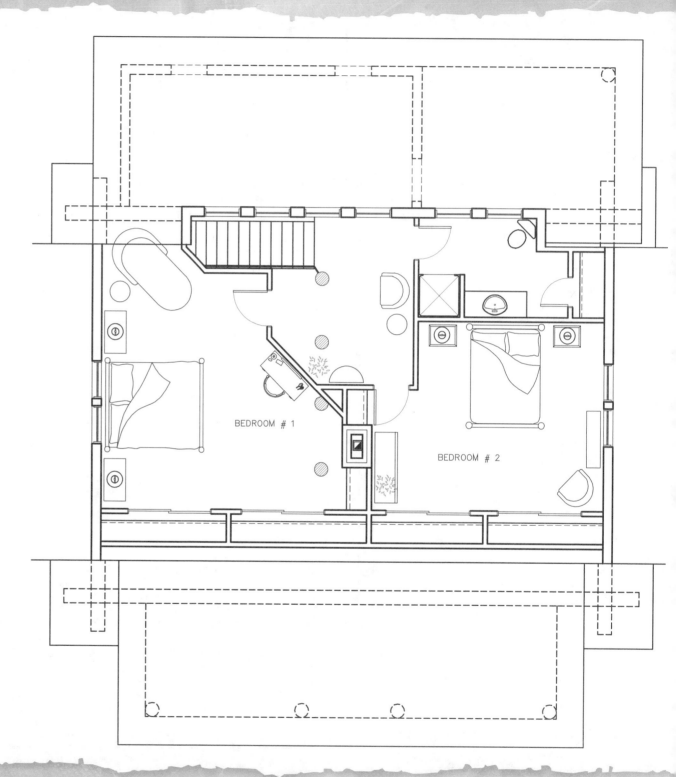

BEDROOM # 1

BEDROOM # 2

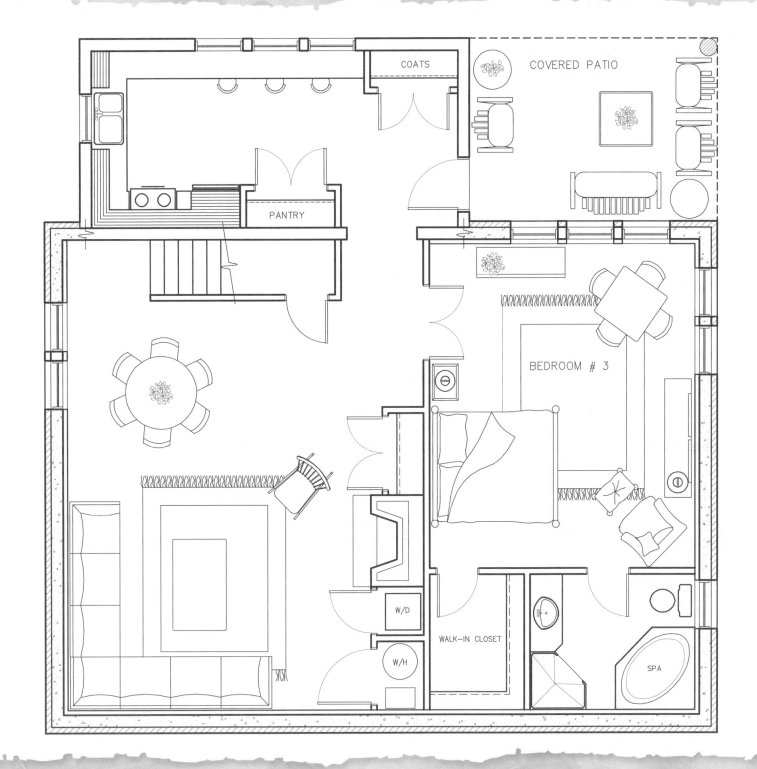

COATS

COVERED PATIO

PANTRY

BEDROOM # 3

W/D

WALK-IN CLOSET

SPA

W/H

Eagle's Nest

Main Floor: 1,540 square feet

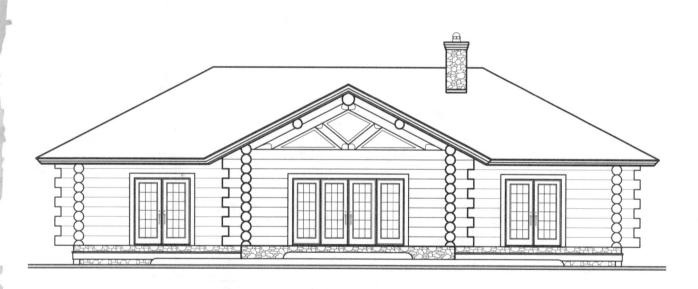

Perched on a mountain with panoramic views overlooking a local ski resort, this log home was designed for one-floor living. The hip-roof design helps reduce the costs associated with standard log gable ends and shrinkage detail. Additional advantages are that the long-line roof appears less "boxy," and the conventionally built roof enables the concealment of a lot of extra lighting, ceiling fans, wiring, and mechanicals that usually take more thought and planning in a log home.

This home features three covered porches. The owner incorporated bear paw prints set into the concrete of the entrance porch for a clever touch of whimsy. The main entry's porch also features a ceiling with small log saplings set side by side to create a great deal of interest and texture while entering the impressive and roomy vestibule. Inside the door is a log bench to sit on while removing winter clothes and boots after coming off the ski slopes. The entry floor is beautiful natural-slate with an etched inlay of a rug border.

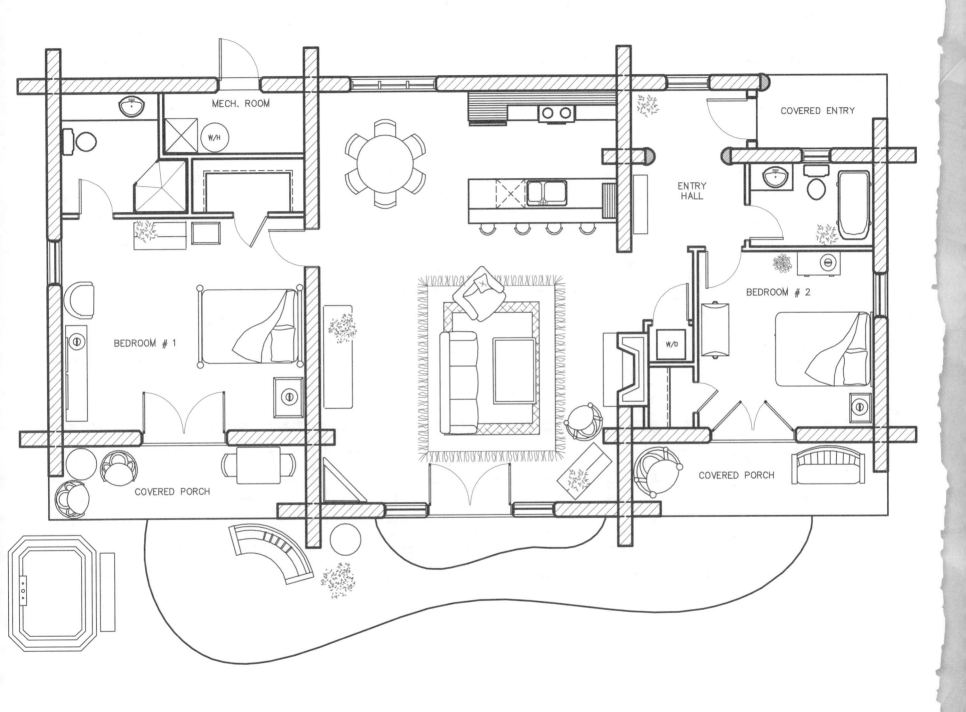

MECH. ROOM

W/H

COVERED ENTRY

ENTRY
HALL

BEDROOM # 1

BEDROOM # 2

W/D

COVERED PORCH

COVERED PORCH

The living room is vaulted fifteen feet with massive log web trusses and purlins. The kitchen, dining room, and master bedroom have large log joists overhead that drop to a ten-foot ceiling. The room's different ceiling heights add to the drama of this log home. The tongue-and-groove walls were used as dividing walls, providing a durable finish for ski-country living.

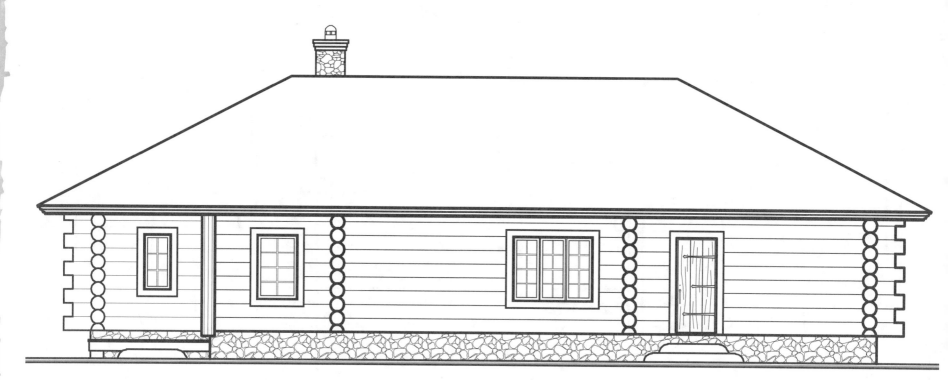

Not only was considerable time put into the layout of this home, but the owner put years of thought and planning into the finishing touches of the 1,540-square-foot getaway retreat, giving it the feel of a luxurious and spacious grand lodge.

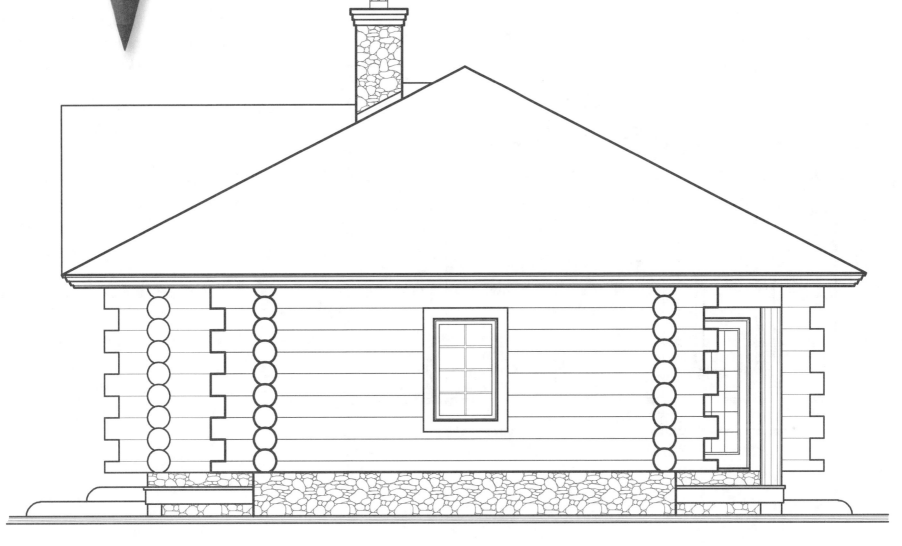

Coyote Run

Main Floor: 1,053 square feet

This unique and charming log home swells beyond its dimensions with fluid grace, creating an atmosphere of traditional cabin life. Modern-day conveniences are incorporated to meet both function and beauty. This log home makes a dramatic statement of simplicity.

The open spaces of the living room and kitchen have a cozy inviting feel. All common areas are within view of the warm glow of the fireplace. The kitchen's placement is part of the living area, so you don't feel trapped away in a secluded location. The outside covered entry porch adds even more living and dining room space, making it a great area to spend a sunny day or starlit evening.

The two bedrooms and two full baths give plenty of private space. A stacked washer and dryer are conveniently located in a hallway closet. The mechanical room is in a garden-style shed attached to the back side of the log structure.

This home gives the feeling of having stepped back in time to an Old West miner's cabin, simple in form and classic in design.

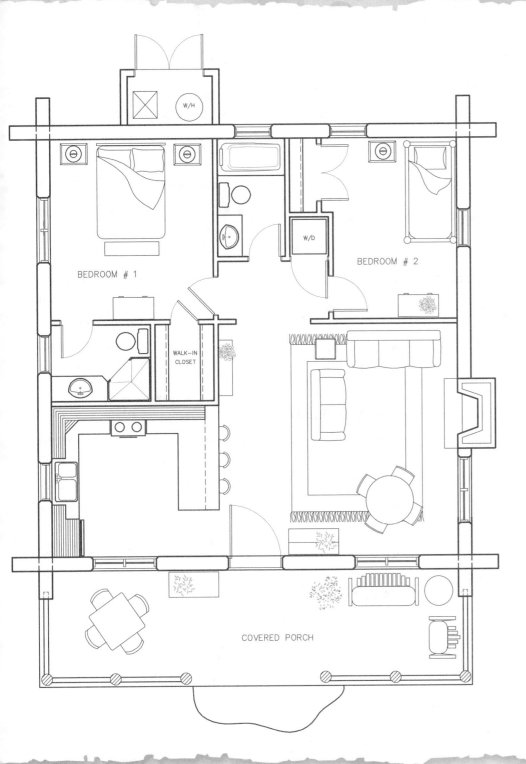

BEDROOM # 1

W/H

W/D

BEDROOM # 2

WALK-IN
CLOSET

COVERED PORCH

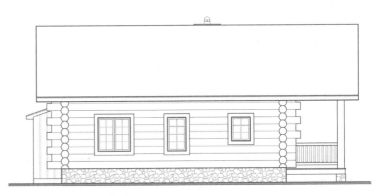

Acorn Ridge

Main Floor: 1,197 square feet

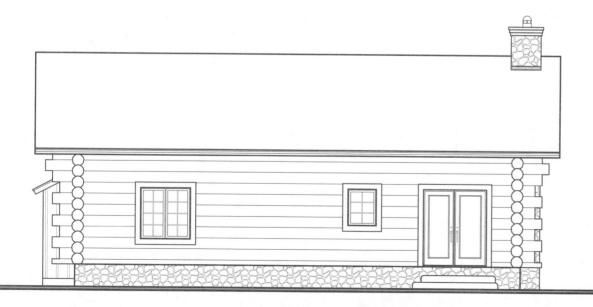

This log home has an entry that welcomes all with its sweeping archway of log timbers supporting the porch's ridge beam. This is a home reminiscent of those found in the rustic northern camps of the Adirondack Mountains and truly captures the simplistic beauty of a traditional log home. This home's best feature is that it is cost-effective in both design and material content.

This home will easily accommodate the first-time homebuyer, small family, empty nester, or vacationers. The ten-foot ceilings use height and light with the backdrop of white sheetrock ceilings to make the space feel bigger. This home's style is a low-maintenance design with all the necessary conveniences but without all the added trappings of life.

The semi-open floor plan allows enjoyment of the fireplace from the living room, dining room, and kitchen. A hallway closet houses

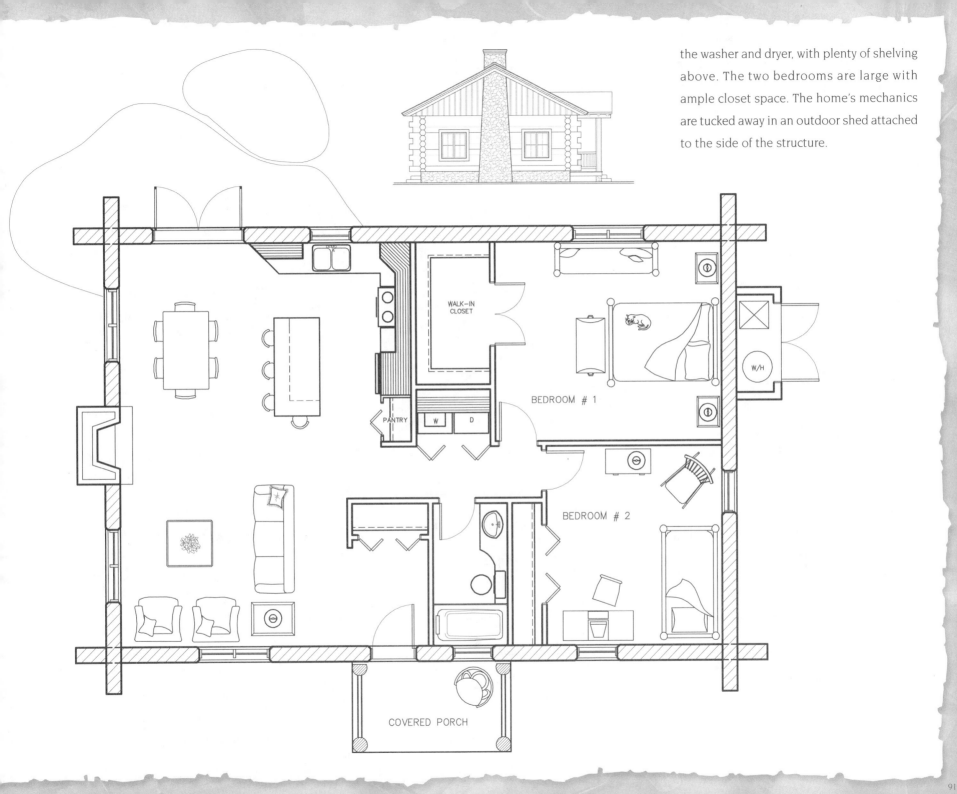

the washer and dryer, with plenty of shelving above. The two bedrooms are large with ample closet space. The home's mechanics are tucked away in an outdoor shed attached to the side of the structure.

WALK-IN CLOSET

PANTRY

W D

BEDROOM # 1

W/H

BEDROOM # 2

COVERED PORCH

Forest Hill Camp

Main Floor: 1,008 square feet

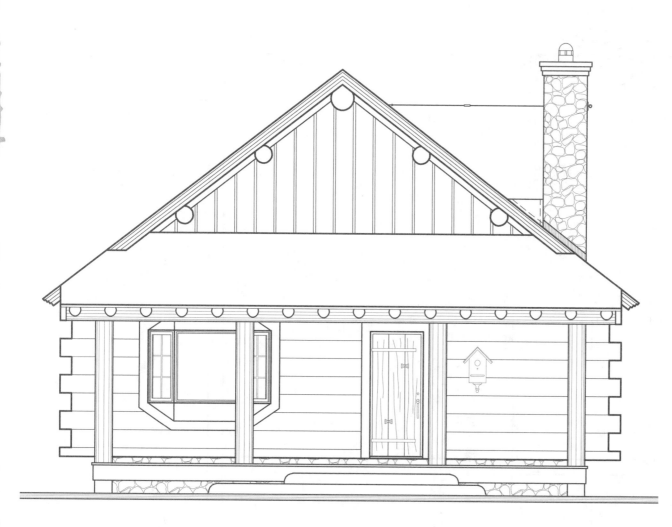

This log home is well thought out, making efficient use of limited space. It has ample room to entertain a small group of family or friends both indoors and out. It is the essence of log cabin living, pared down to basic comforts for a cost-effective and affordable structure.

The kitchen is the center of activity with a wraparound layout and the bonus of a large pantry for extra cabin provisions. The kitchen's bay-window breakfast bar, with a great view of the outdoors, can be turned into a work counter for kids' school projects.

The living room is spacious and comfortable, incorporating a fireplace that takes the chill off even the coldest of winter nights, with an area for a sit-down dinner or a late-night game of cards by the crackling fire.

The two bedrooms are large with plenty of closet space. For the occasional overnight guests, a foldaway sofa bed in front of the fireplace will do. This log home design has a calming environment with a touch of the forest inside.

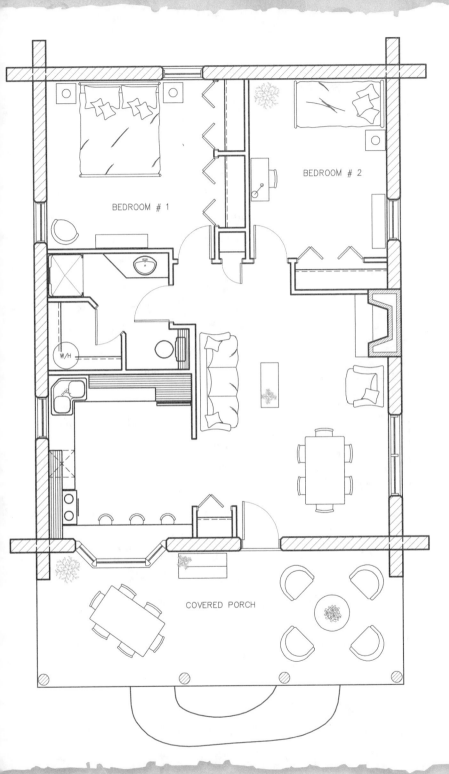

BEDROOM # 1

BEDROOM # 2

W/H

COVERED PORCH

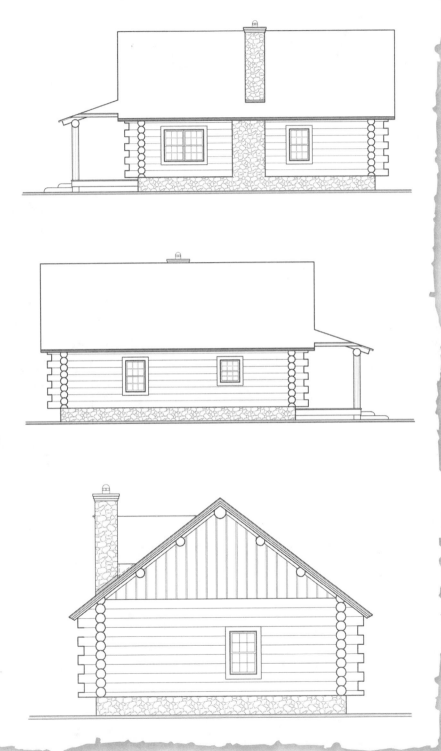

Love's Cove

Main Floor: 770 square feet • Basement: 730 square feet (daylight)

This design embodies the true spirit and romance of the log home's pure simplicity. Included are two versions of the plan to illustrate how a plan can easily be reversed (see page 37). There is a panoramic view from wraparound bay windows, which have been thoughtfully designed to create a built-in dining nook that captures the natural outside environment.

The floor plan's fluid movement of space creates a peaceful and restful home with its informal design. The oversized fireplace is for the romantic soul. The hearth is built with a pass-through storage box for the convenience of not having to carry firewood throughout the house. The kitchen is packed with plenty of cupboards and countertops, as well as a pantry. The main-floor master bedroom suite is large, with a private bathroom.

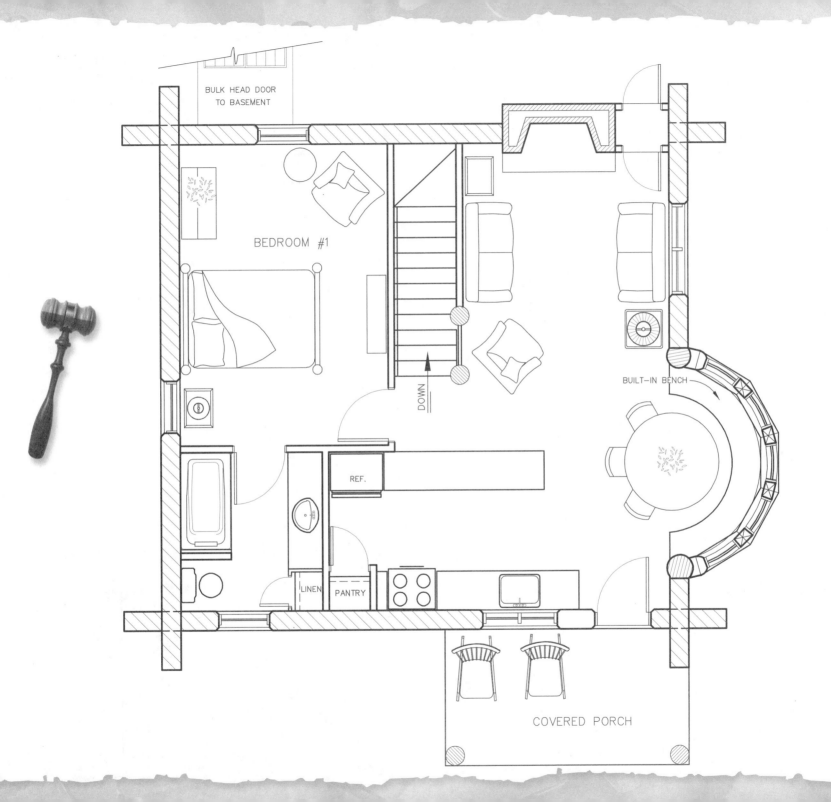

BULK HEAD DOOR
TO BASEMENT

BEDROOM #1

DOWN

BUILT-IN BENCH

REF.

LINEN

PANTRY

COVERED PORCH

95

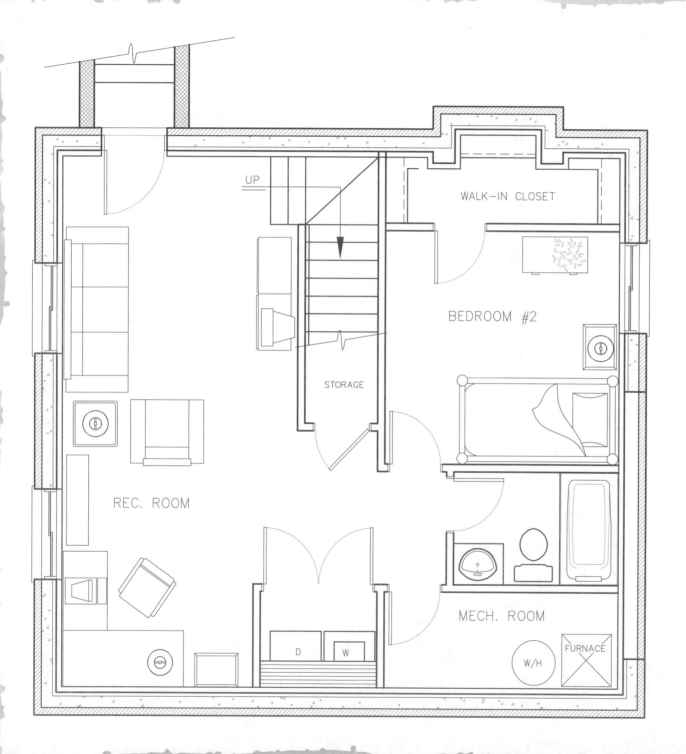

UP

WALK-IN CLOSET

BEDROOM #2

STORAGE

REC. ROOM

MECH. ROOM

D   W

W/H   FURNACE

This small log home doubles in size by making use of its full basement with a large recreation room, laundry area, extra bedroom, walk-in closet, and another full bath. This home's design is a true exercise in efficiency and grace.

The roof's sculptural form was created with conventionally built trusses for a cost-effective design. There are large decorative log joists in this home's interior ceiling that create even more rustic charm without adding the full expense of a vaulted log-roof system. A gracefully designed log-scissors truss in the front entry creates an environment that is a great place for rocking chairs and large glasses of iced tea.

Turtle Hill Camp

Main Floor: 495 square feet

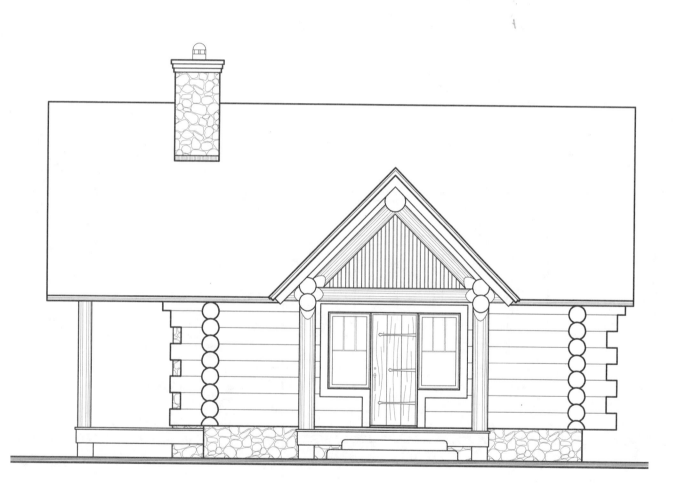

This is a perfect guest house, holiday getaway, or weekend cabin for two that has the bare essentials and requires few materials to build, enabling you to own a camp without it owning you. We built a similar version of this log cabin hideaway on an island where guests and our adult children can truly feel they have a place of their own to stay. The cabin was created over many years with leftovers, salvaged materials, flea-market funk, and junkyard finds.

Although petite in footprint, it is big in spirit. From tree house to dream house, it is where real life and fantasy converge. The log cabin is loaded with storybook charm and great curb appeal.

The entry-porch design has the detailed rhythm of small log spindles incorporated into its truss. The side porch is large, extending the exterior living space with the added luxury of a fireplace, making it a great outdoor room.

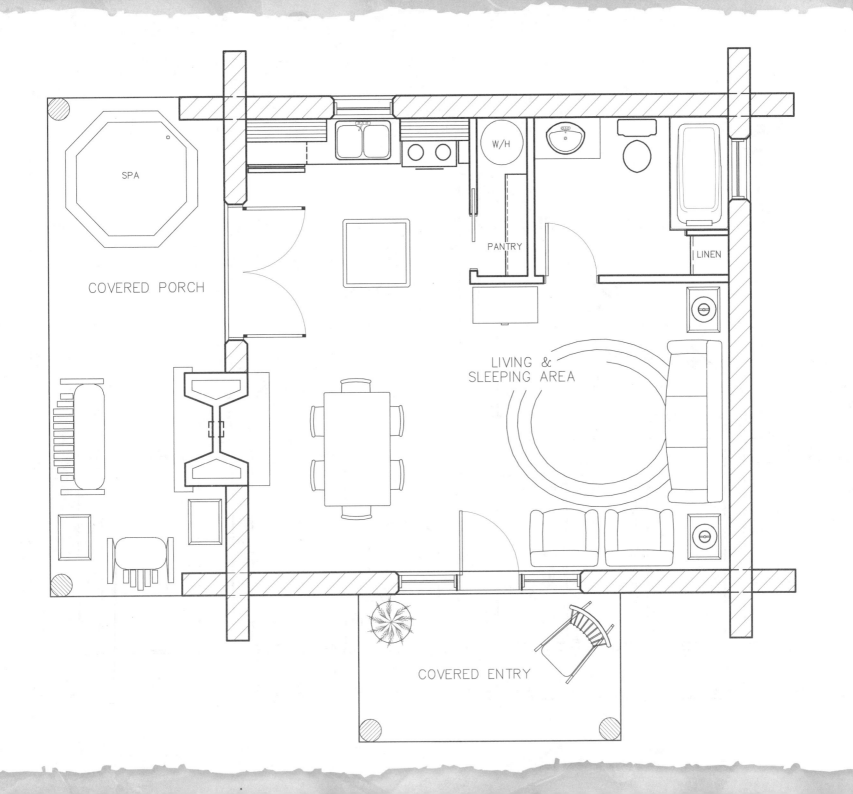

SPA

COVERED PORCH

W/H

PANTRY

LINEN

LIVING &
SLEEPING AREA

COVERED ENTRY

The indoor area is an open concept of shared spaces that soar with a vaulted log-purlin ceiling, bringing in additional light from the full gable-end window to chase away the winter blues.

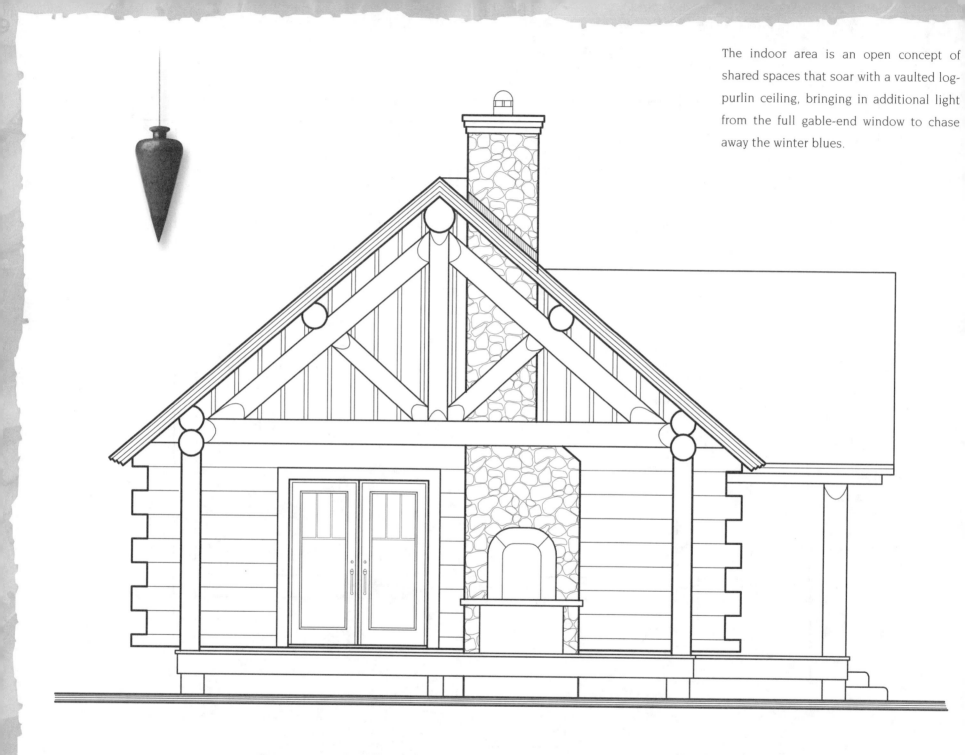

Red Hook Bluff

Main Floor: 1,380 *square feet*

This is a spin-off of a very popular design called Coldwater Creek, featured in the book Small Log Homes. A recent client took that plan and requested some modifications to fit his needs for his retirement home that was set on a Montana hilltop.

The client ultimately decided to design the home with a conventionally framed wall system, then incorporated log elements and accents. Although the log-element design was a very successful and beautiful look, I wanted to share the log home version of it here.

This is a log home designed for outdoor living with endless covered porches. The peaked covered porch directs visitors to the main entry, while the side porch has the magic of an outdoor fireplace, perfect for many outdoor activities.

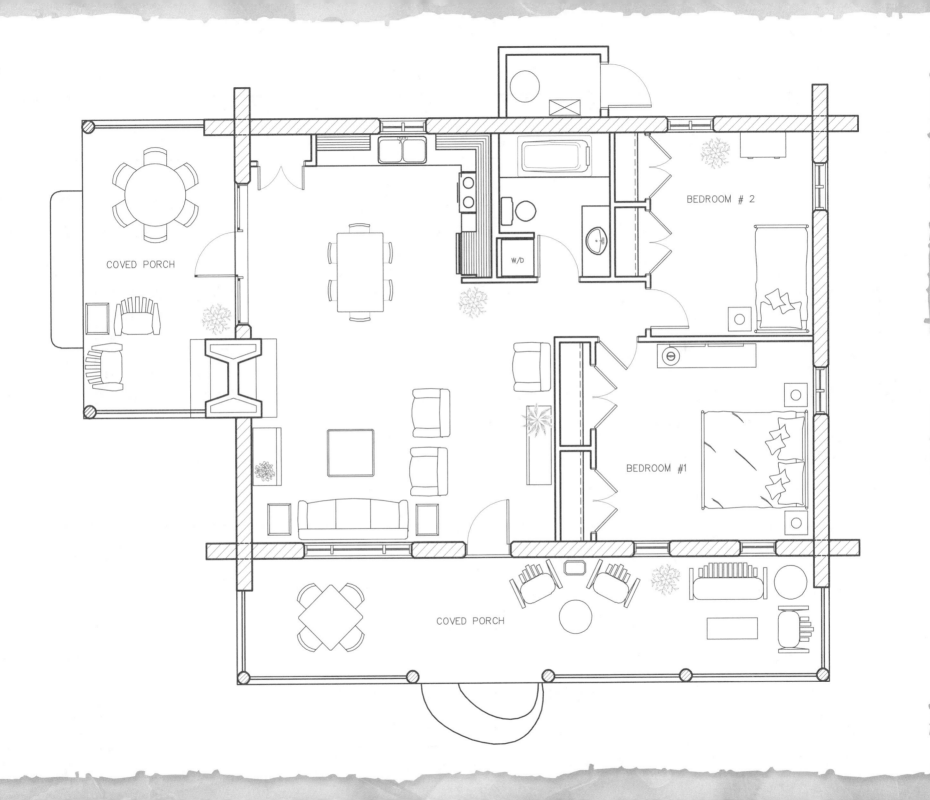

COVED PORCH

W/D

BEDROOM # 2

BEDROOM #1

COVED PORCH

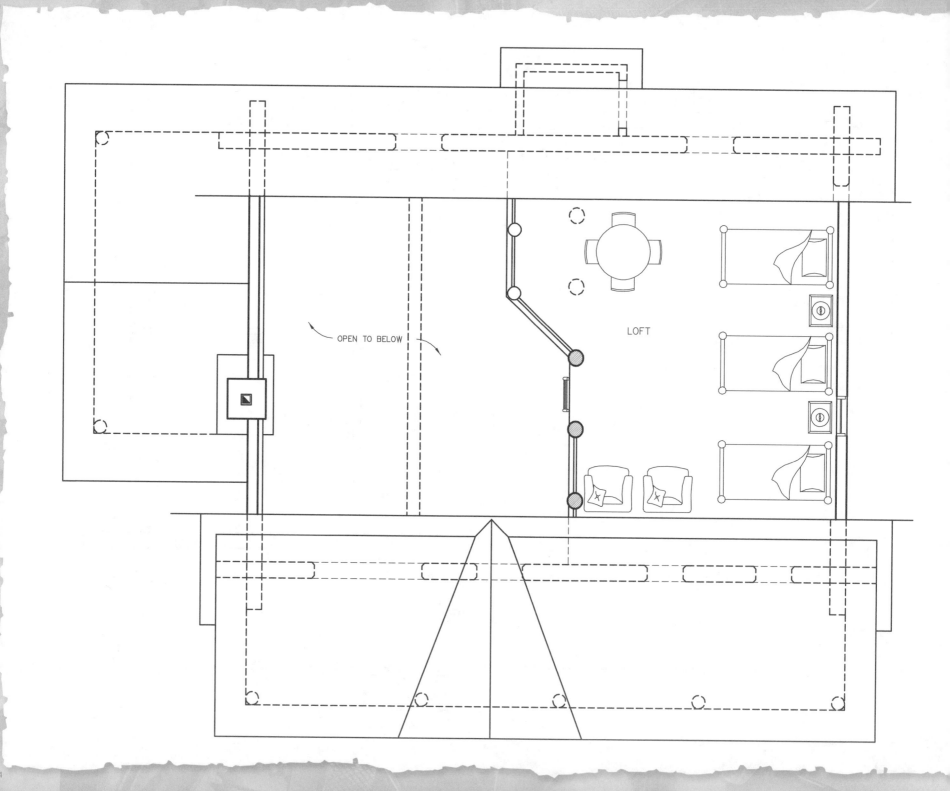

OPEN TO BELOW

LOFT

The indoor fireplace is the focus of the central living area. The kitchen, dining room, living room, and bunk loft feature massive log purlins, ridgepoles, and trusses in the exposed roof system. There are two good-sized bedrooms on the first floor that also have large log-ceiling joists and are designed with his-and-her closets. The upstairs loft can be used for an additional bunkroom, library, or office.

Moonlight Bay

Main Floor: 1,211 square feet • Basement: 728 square feet (walkout)

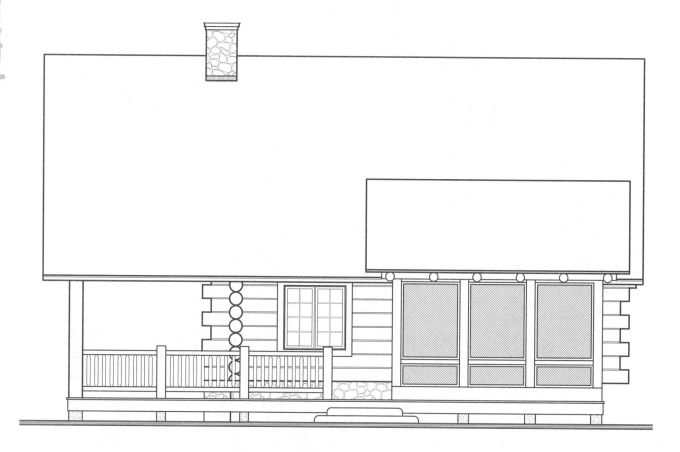

This log home is designed for those who love entertaining outdoors. There is a mix of covered and screened-in porches as well as sunny decks. They are each large areas with plenty of room for those summer afternoon barbecues with friends and family. The oversized living room incorporates French doors that invite the landscape inside. Because of the large covered porch outside the living room and kitchen areas, the doors can be left wide open even during a heavy summer's rain. The country kitchen is large enough to incorporate a dining table. The extra-large pantry could house an army of dry goods and equipment.

The upstairs master suite creates a private getaway. This large bedroom incorporates a dormer window to expand its size. The log purlins in the bedroom and bath's roof system soar above with vaulted peaks.

The bonus of a walkout basement adds a lot more space for an additional guestroom suite or a "kids' camp" with plenty of closet space for young adults. This basement flat can separate and conceal all the added noise

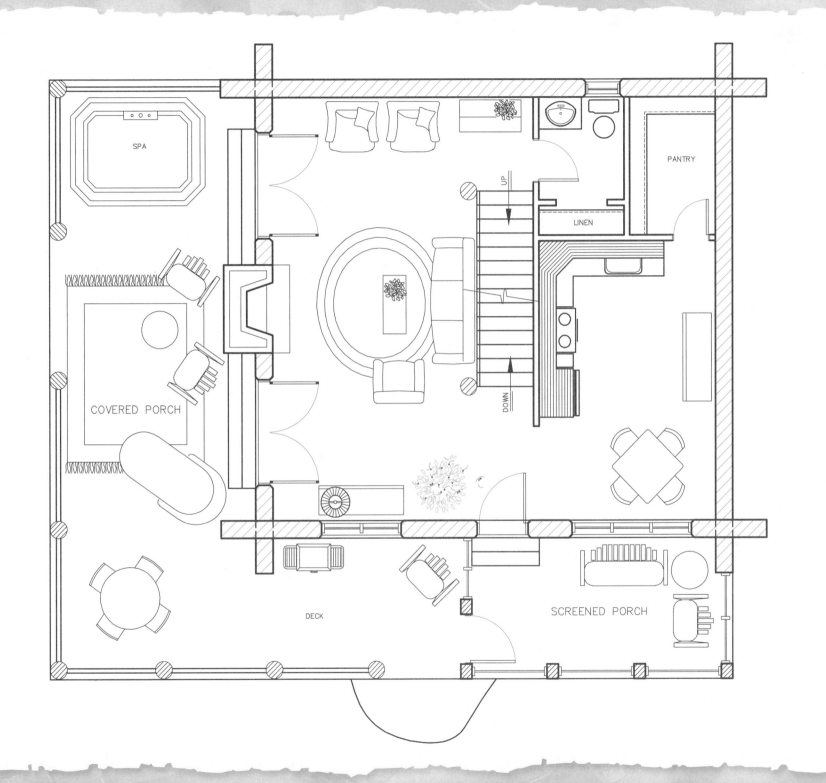

SPA

PANTRY

UP

LINEN

COVERED PORCH

DOWN

DECK

SCREENED PORCH

and mess that seems to appear from no-where. Also, the washer and dryer are conveniently located for kids who enjoy helping with family wash privileges.

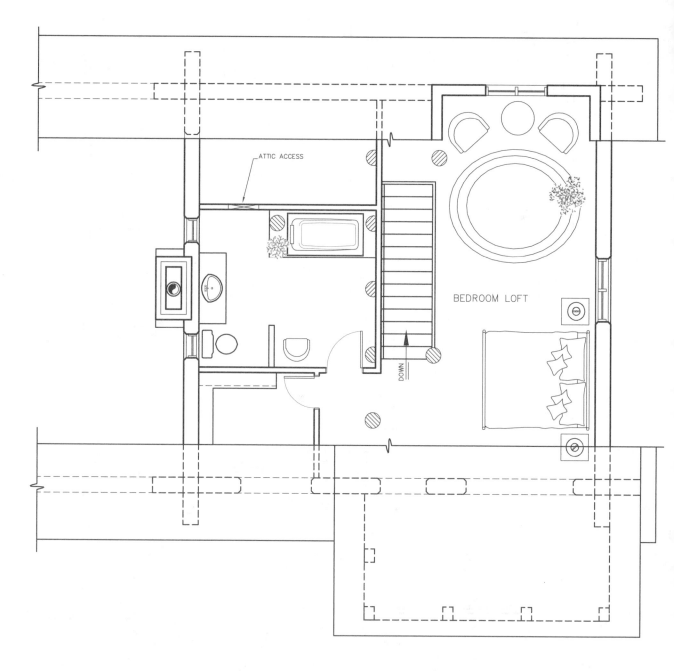

ATTIC ACCESS

BEDROOM LOFT

DOWN

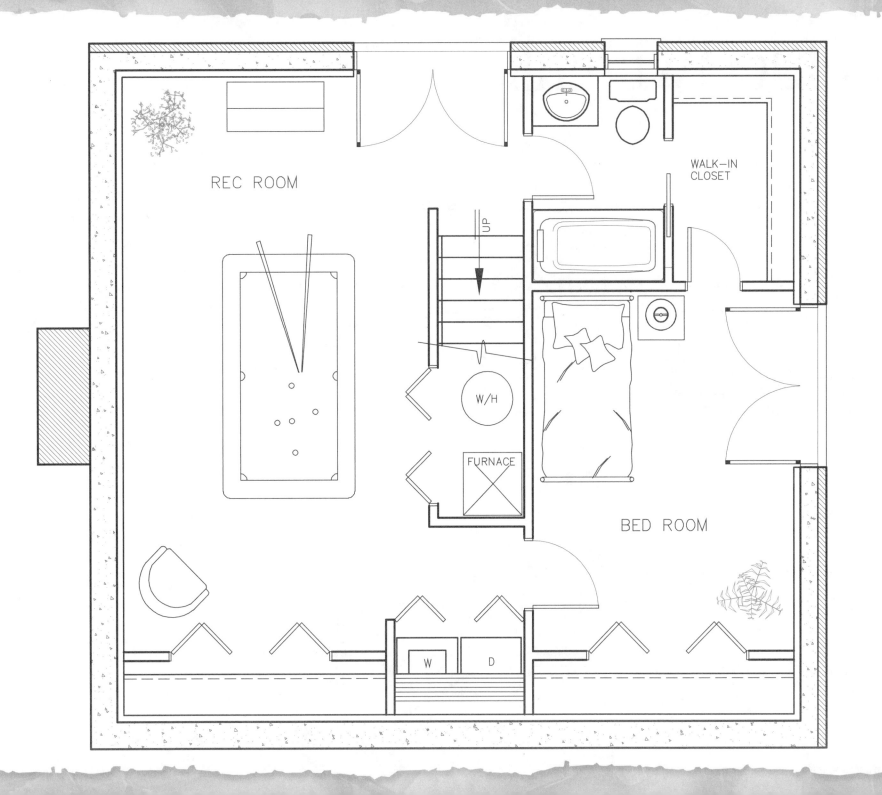

REC ROOM

WALK-IN
CLOSET

UP

W/H

FURNACE

BED ROOM

W   D

Celtic Twilight

Main Floors: 2,118 square feet • Basement: 1,868 square feet (with garage)

This architect designed an elegant log home lodge classic where the intersection of log walls is a work of art. The sense of spaciousness makes this home as dramatic inside as it is outside. Its covered porch draws you inside to an entry hall bench where you can sit and remove your shoes. The entry hall opens into a classic country kitchen. The spacious living room and old-fashioned, oversized fireplace radiate the warmth of log home living. There is the bonus of a private loft tucked above the kitchen, which overlooks the large living room below.

Three oversized bedrooms are tailored for one-floor living. The master bedroom suite is an elegant refuge with a wonderful walk-in closet and master bathroom. The conventional roof system above the bedroom wings allows for a lot of space within the bedroom ceiling to house all types of lighting, speaker systems, and large ductwork. This log home incorporates real log gable ends that are

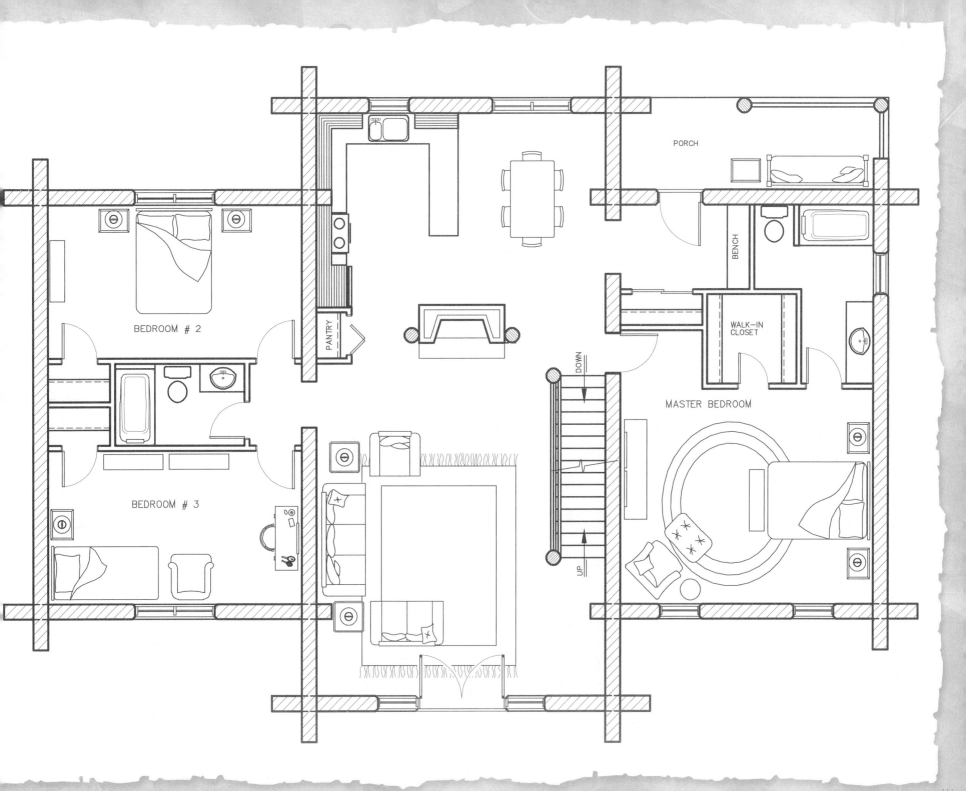

PORCH

PANTRY

BEDROOM # 2

BEDROOM # 3

BENCH

DOWN

UP

WALK-IN CLOSET

MASTER BEDROOM

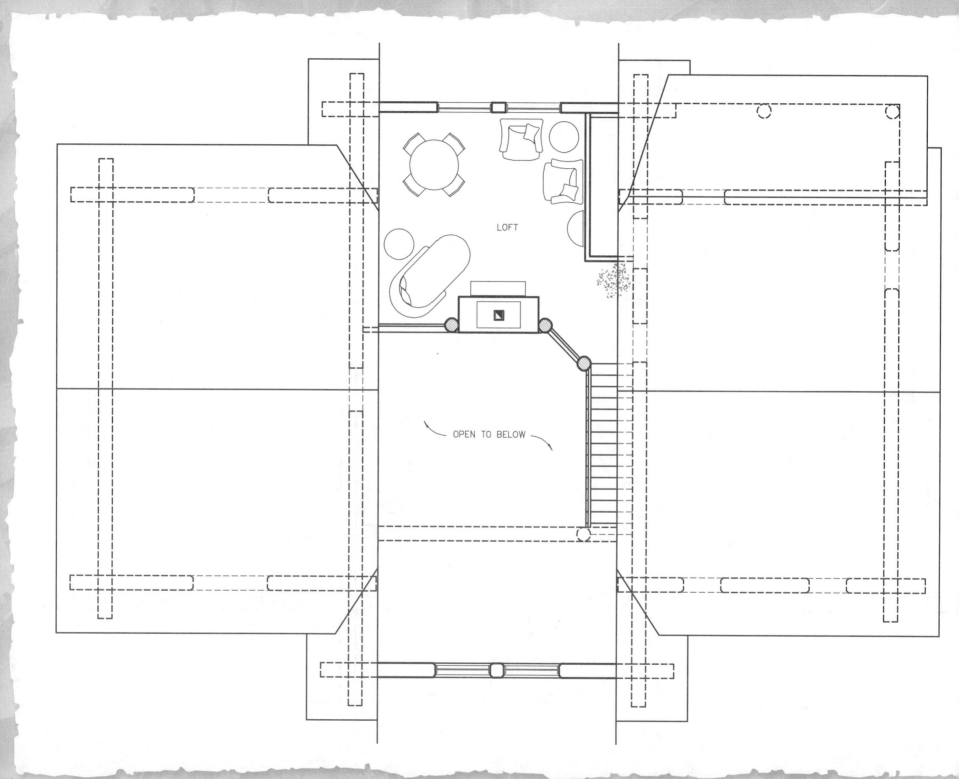

LOFT

OPEN TO BELOW

carefully braced and calculated for the allowances needed for shrinkage of the gable ends.

The client requested an open basement plan for future development. The basement incorporates a two-car garage, laundry room, bathroom, utility room, and oversized workshop. With some additional planning, this large basement can be transformed into whatever the heart desires.

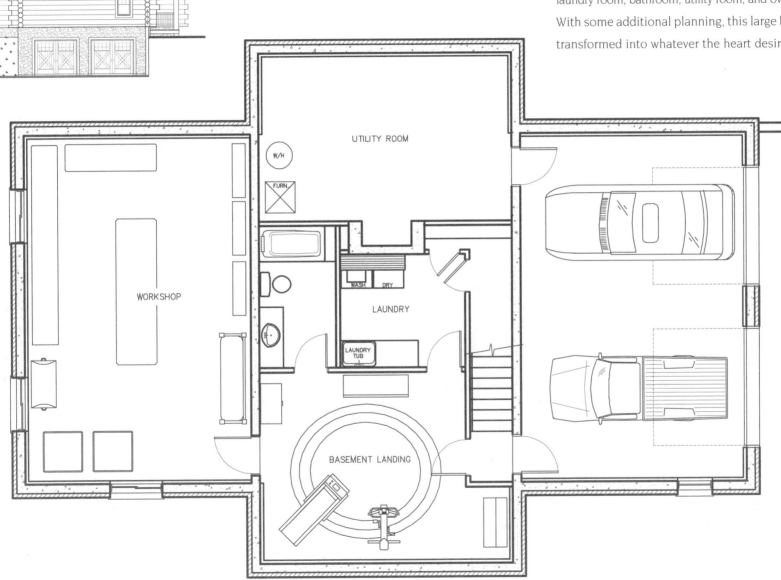

UTILITY ROOM

W/H

FURN.

WORKSHOP

WASH   DRY

LAUNDRY

LAUNDRY
TUB

BASEMENT LANDING

Whispering Pines

Main Floors: 1,800 square feet • Basement: 1,100 square feet (walkout)

This home's most striking feature is its dramatic roof angles and dormers that add great curb appeal from any angle. It is a stimulating atmosphere created for the family with a passion for outdoor living. The four-season sunroom with cottage charm adds warmth to any season. The porch wraps around the home, and an artful mix of decks, patios, covered porches, and screen porches prepares for the time of year when mosquitoes seem to become as big as birds.

The multipurpose floor plan with design flexibility allows for both open spaces and quiet hideaways. The kitchen has an efficient work triangle with a modern-day butler's pantry that incorporates the washer and dryer near the kitchen's work center. With small modifications to the first-floor library and bathroom, there is the possibility of creating a senior master-bedroom suite for future one-floor living. The double-sided fireplace can be viewed from the dining room, living room, and sunroom, and there

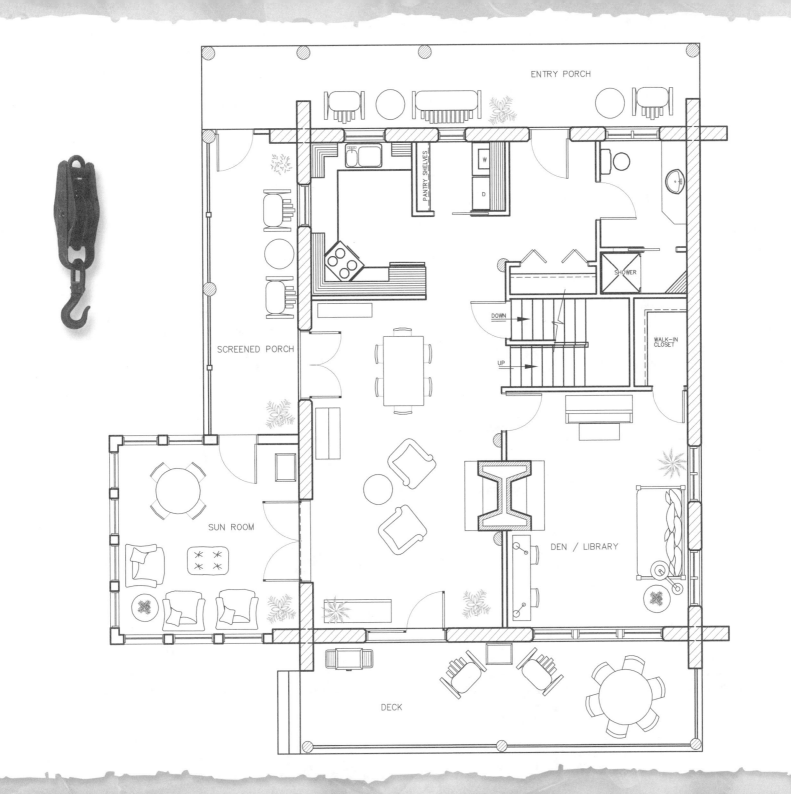

ENTRY PORCH

PANTRY SHELVES

SCREENED PORCH

SHOWER

DOWN

UP

WALK-IN CLOSET

SUN ROOM

DEN / LIBRARY

DECK

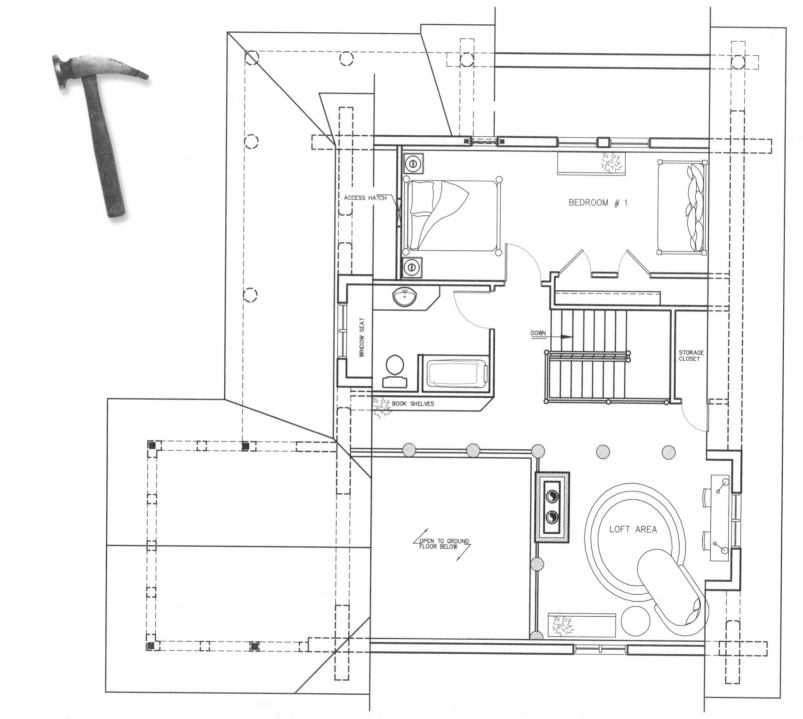

ACCESS HATCH

BEDROOM # 1

WINDOW SEAT

DOWN

STORAGE CLOSET

BOOK SHELVES

OPEN TO GROUND FLOOR BELOW

LOFT AREA

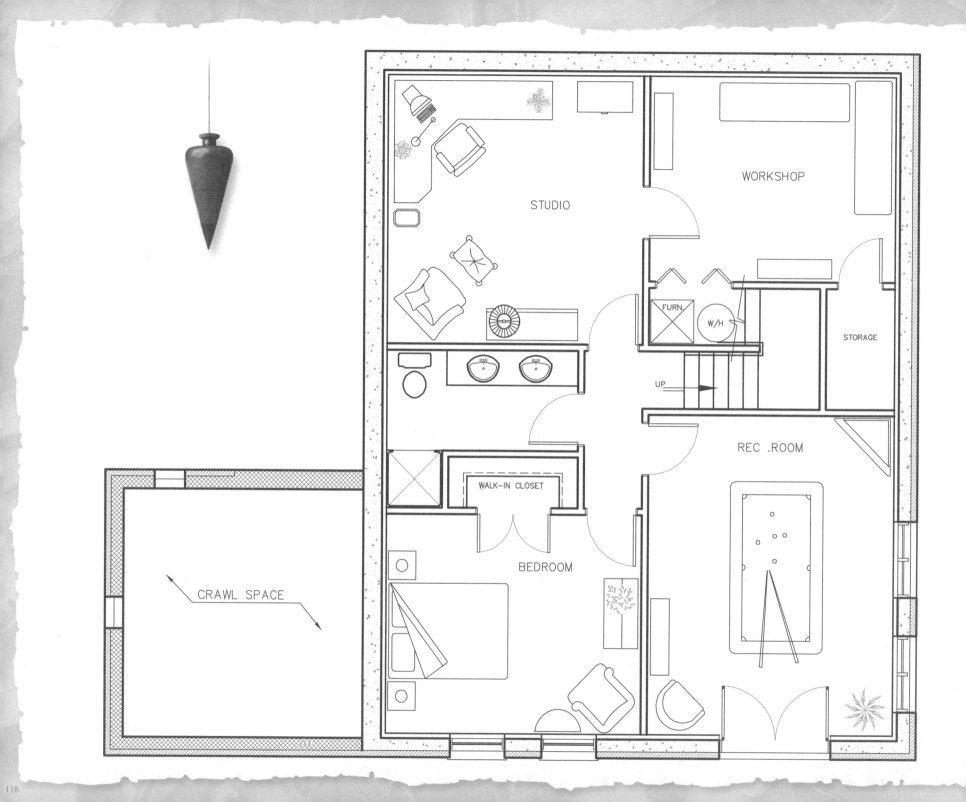

STUDIO

WORKSHOP

FURN.

W/H

STORAGE

UP

REC .ROOM

WALK-IN CLOSET

BEDROOM

CRAWL SPACE

is also a separate firebox in the library. This log home incorporates so many windows that there is a dance of light throughout the day.

On the second floor is a secluded bedroom. The bathroom makes good use of a dormer with an added special touch: a window seat that stores linen below. An isolated loft is tucked away over the living area, with another dormer that opens up to the area, allowing the maximum amount of usable space and light. Throughout this home there are structural elements of the log-roof system that are exposed for all to enjoy.

Other amenities include a walkout basement with an additional bedroom, full bath, workshop, studio, and recreation room with French doors that exit onto an outdoor patio. The layout is perfect for a log home nestled into rock-ledge outcroppings or a hillside, tying it to the land.

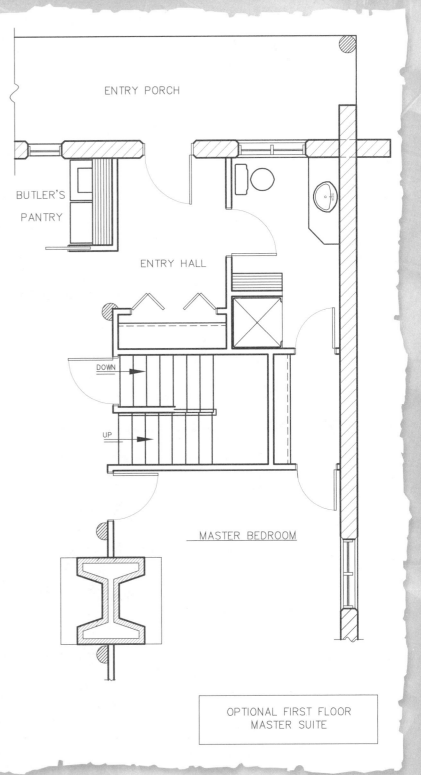

ENTRY PORCH

BUTLER'S PANTRY

ENTRY HALL

DOWN

UP

MASTER BEDROOM

OPTIONAL FIRST FLOOR
MASTER SUITE

Wolf Lodge

Main Floors: 3,124 square feet (with garage)

This log home is what dreams are made of.
The home has character no matter what angle you view it from. This architect's years of experience show in the level of detail incorporated into the dance of logs intersecting throughout the structure. The sophisticated use of log joinery goes beyond the log walls and into the roof system, engineered for massive snow loads.

The home has an air-lock entry that leads into a large foyer, then spills over into an elegant living room with large log columns that add to the room's architectural interest. There is a mix of covered porches and outdoor decks that add more scenic rooms. The kitchen and dining room both have their own nooks carved out of the intersection of logs. A guest bathroom and a laundry room are conveniently located off the two-car garage.

The first floor has a master bedroom suite with a private bathroom. This master suite could also easily be transformed into a

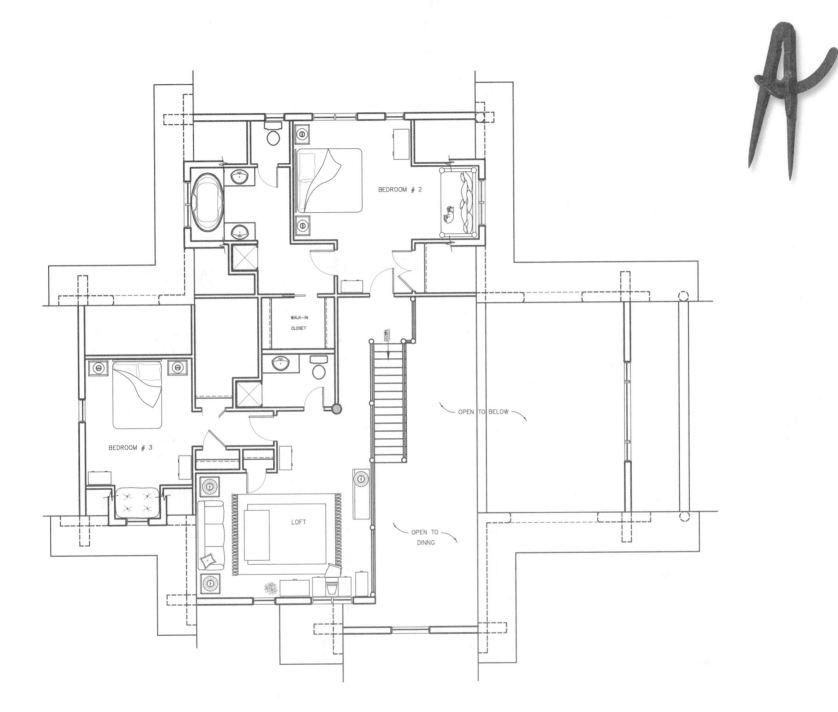

BEDROOM # 2

BEDROOM # 3

WALK-IN
CLOSET

DOWN

OPEN TO BELOW

LOFT

OPEN TO
DINNG

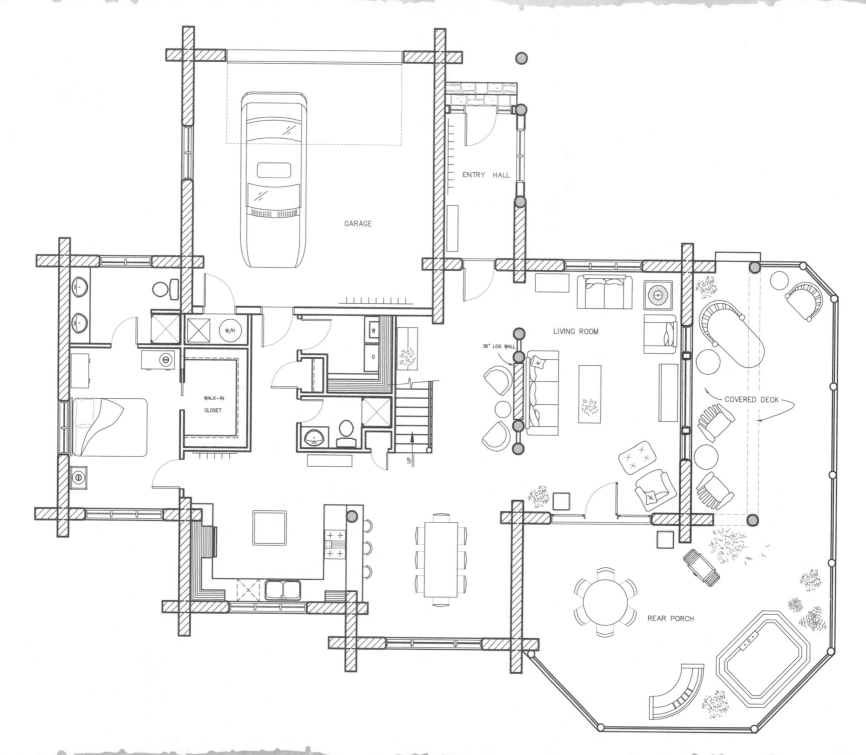

GARAGE

ENTRY HALL

LIVING ROOM

38" LOG WALL

COVERED DECK

WALK-IN
CLOSET

W/H

W

D

UP

REAR PORCH

first-floor office space with its own side-door entry by making a few changes to the design.

The loft's conversation nook has wonderful views of the living room and dining room below. There is a third bedroom tucked into the back wing of the loft, as well as a second master bedroom suite. The poetry of inter-secting log work and multiple dormers creates storybook character and creative charm in this log home estate.

Moss Hill

Main Floors: 2,130 *square feet* • Basement: 1,278 *square feet*

This is a great home design for entertaining guests. The open living/dining/great room area extends itself in the warm weather months by using the covered porch for outdoor living. A central masonry fireplace with a built-in pizza oven makes an efficient heating system for this home. The master suite is spacious, with plenty of closets for extra clothes, linen, and storage. The master bathroom has an added bonus of a wrap-around spa with windows that give the impression of being outside. With a modification to the floor plan, this area could also be used as a shower bay for those who have a private location.

Upstairs are two bedrooms with a shared bath and a library loft or hideaway that overlook the great room's conversation area below. The two bedrooms could be made into a second master-bedroom loft. The one-and-a-half-story design has many intersecting dormers that add interest to the second-floor roof system.

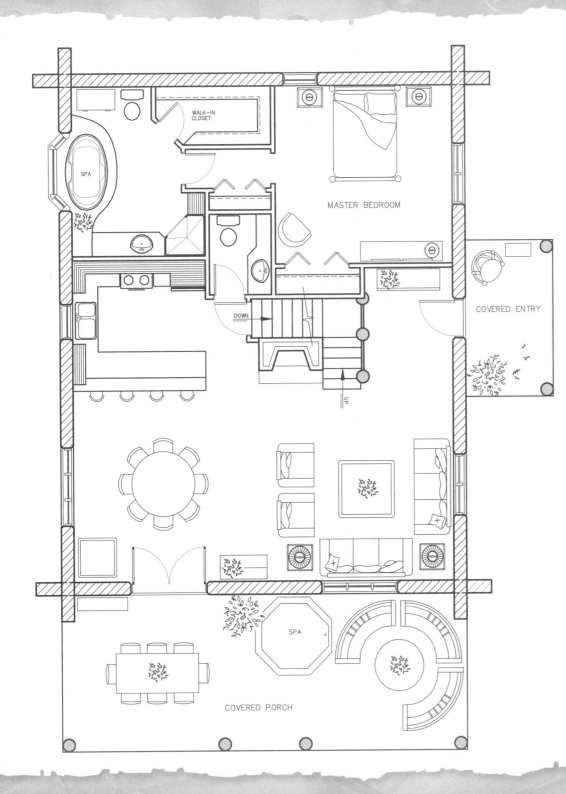

WALK-IN CLOSET

SPA

MASTER BEDROOM

COVERED ENTRY

DOWN

UP

SPA

COVERED PORCH

The basement was created with an abundance of light, making it a cheerful, livable space. Two bedrooms fit downstairs comfortably, with a shared bathroom and many closets and built-in storage. The large media room could also be used to house a pool or Ping-Pong table.

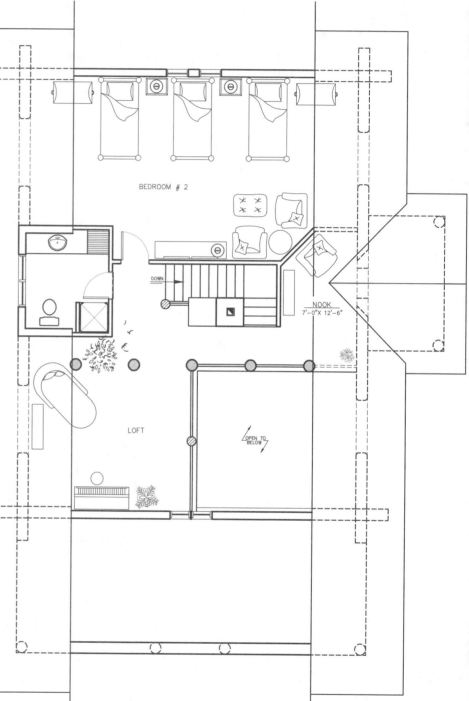

BEDROOM # 2

DOWN

NOOK
7'-0" X 12'-6"

LOFT

OPEN TO
BELOW

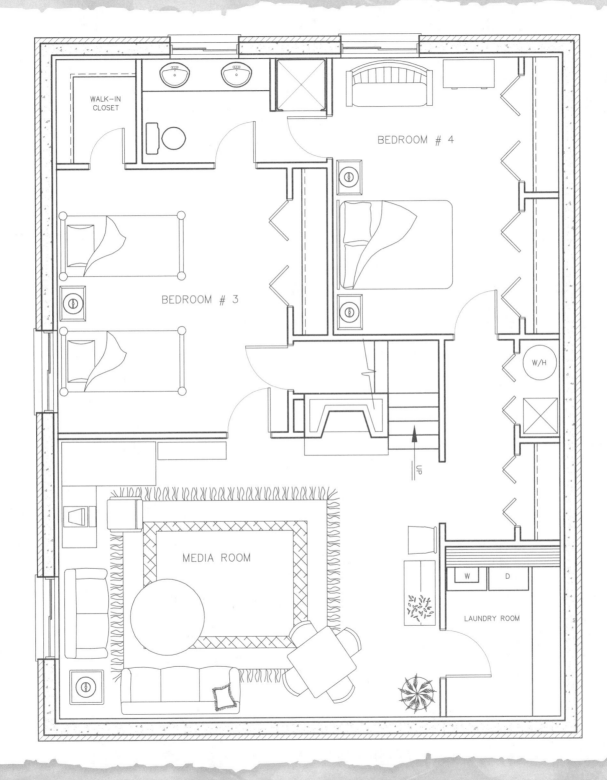

WALK-IN
CLOSET

BEDROOM # 4

BEDROOM # 3

W/H

UP

MEDIA ROOM

W   D

LAUNDRY ROOM

Sugar Bush

Main Floors: 1,415 square feet

This is a Vermont architect's primary residence, a small log home that embodies classic New England charm, and it is filled with striking features. Its screened-in porch's informal entry has a romantic quality. In the mudroom entry, an artfully designed log rail with free-form twig work has a sculptural flair. A small loft serves as the architect's studio. The loft area is multi-functional as an office, library, guest room, or media room.

The dining room has two large banks of windows, giving it a sunroom feel. The kitchen is laid out in a small but efficient galley style. The mudroom has a washer and dryer hidden behind a closet door, plenty of space for all that winter gear, and a bathroom conveniently located close by.

The sugar-bush wood-slat vent on top of the log home's roof system is a whimsical touch as well as a practical but brilliant construction design that deserves more attention. This rooftop vent creates a natural air-conditioning system that, when opened

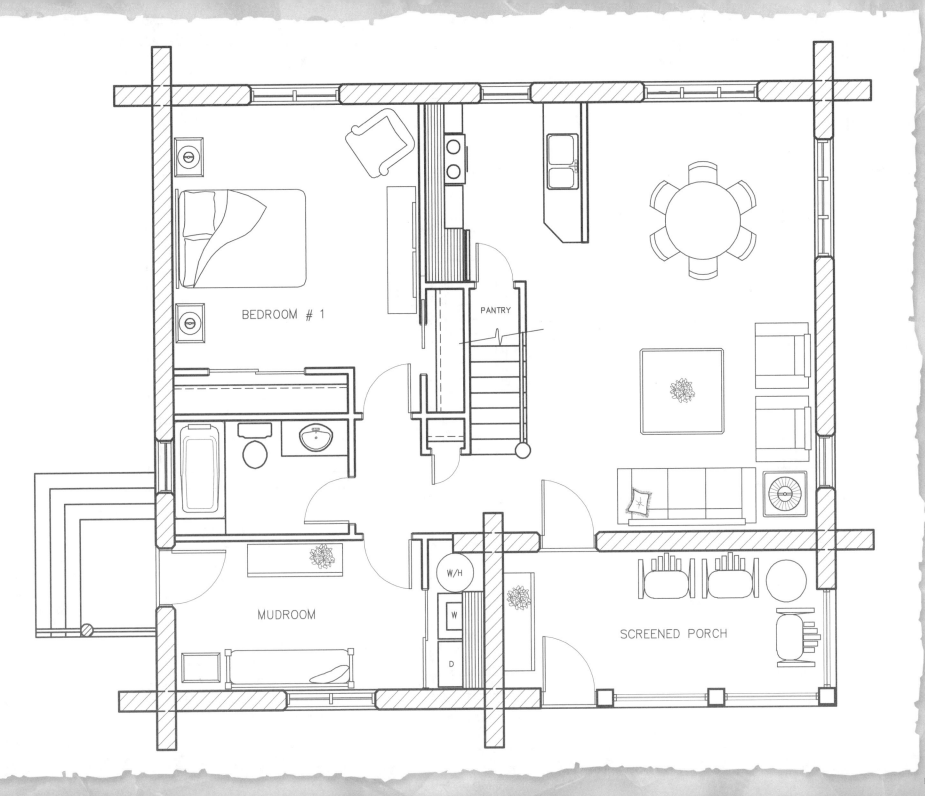

BEDROOM # 1

PANTRY

MUDROOM

W/H

W

D

SCREENED PORCH

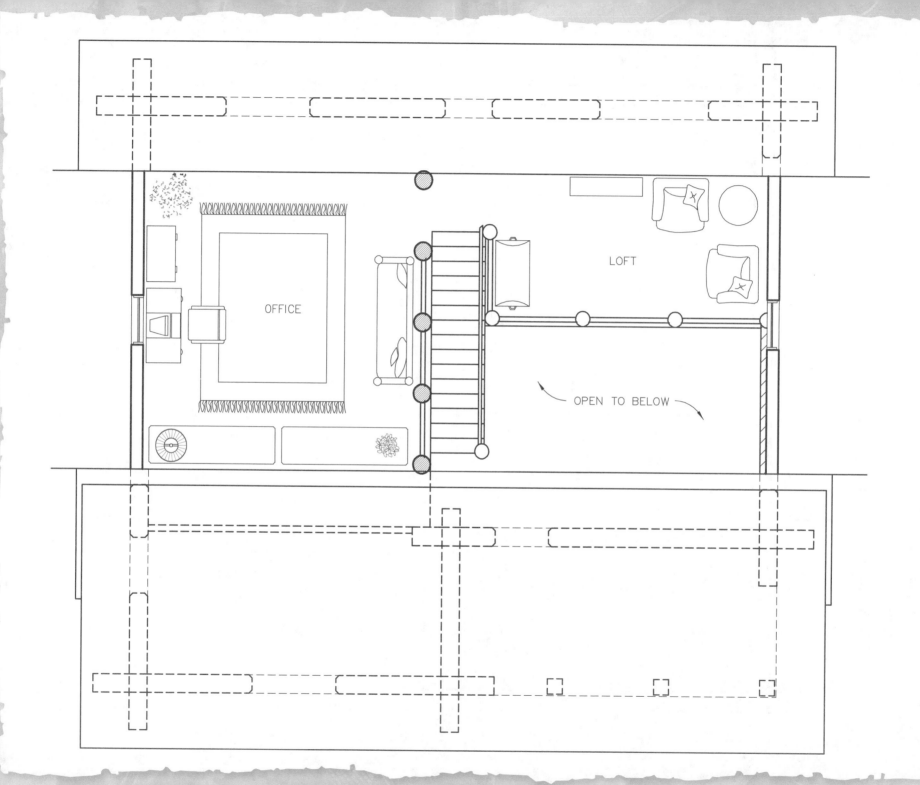

OFFICE

LOFT

OPEN TO BELOW

in the summer, creates a "chimney effect" of cool air that sweeps through the home.

Another smart construction detail worth mentioning is the concrete pier system, used instead of a slab, crawl space, or full foundation. This is a very economical way of building in the North. Funds available for a basement can instead be placed into the home's main living areas where it will be appreciated.

White Pines

Main Floors: 2,198 square feet

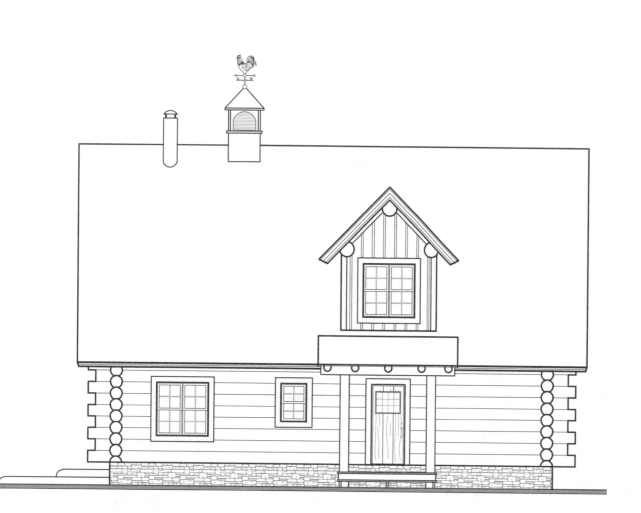

This architect creatively developed a getaway camp with four individual bedrooms for plenty of overnight guests, all within a very modest footprint and designed with every inch carefully considered. The covered porch leads into the home's entry hall with a long bench and closet for all those winter clothes, hats, scarves, and boots. The first floor has a master bedroom with a walk-in closet, as well as an additional bunkroom, shared bathroom, and stacked washer/dryer located in a hallway closet. The open floor plan and light-filled space of the country kitchen and living room wraps around a woodstove. An exterior stone patio adds warm-weather living to this outdoor room accented by nature.

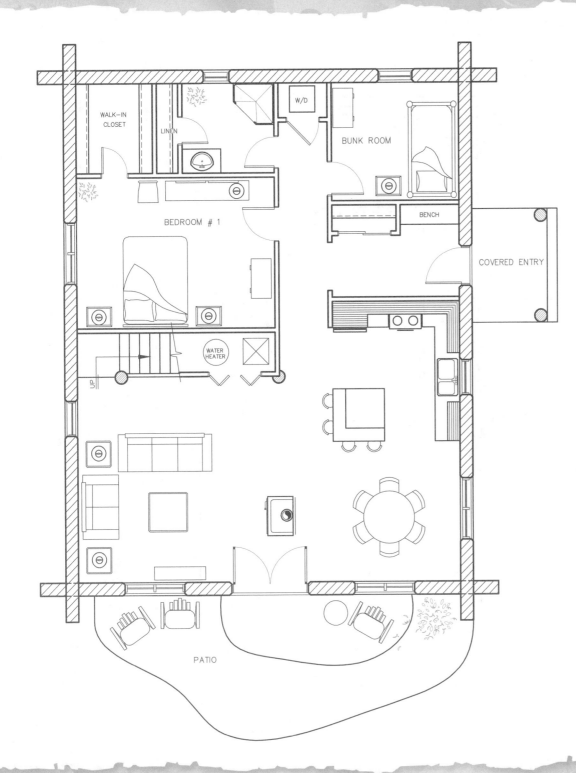

WALK–IN
CLOSET

LINEN

W/D

BUNK ROOM

BEDROOM # 1

BENCH

COVERED ENTRY

WATER
HEATER

UP

PATIO

A staircase with a natural log railing leads to a loft that overlooks the living room. The second-floor open loft is multifunctional and could be used as a game room, den, or hobby area. The upstairs has two bedrooms and a shared bathroom. One of the bedrooms is creatively carved out of a small window dormer. In the bathroom, a large soaking tub is tucked under the roofline. This is a log home designed and built for fun and relaxation, big enough to handle a crowd but small enough to be cozy.

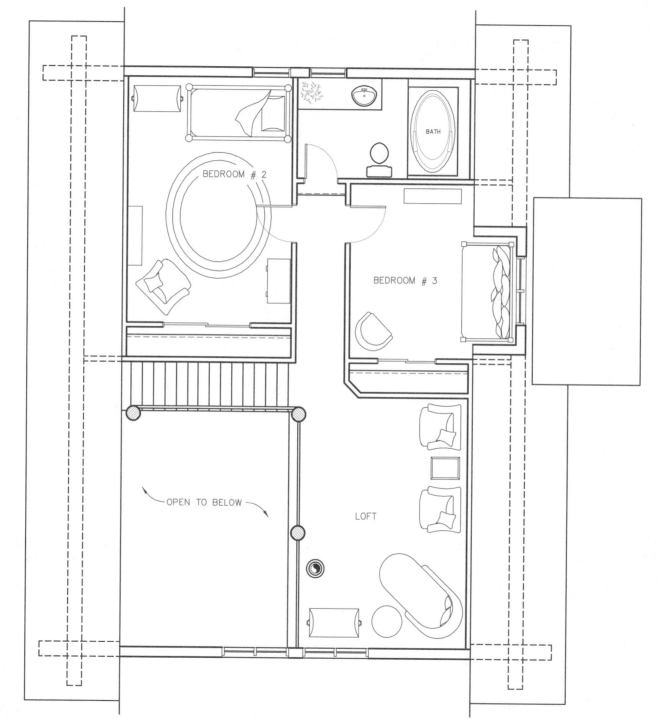

BEDROOM # 2

BATH

BEDROOM # 3

OPEN TO BELOW

LOFT

Apple Wood

Main Floor: 1,915 square feet • Basement: 1,260 square feet

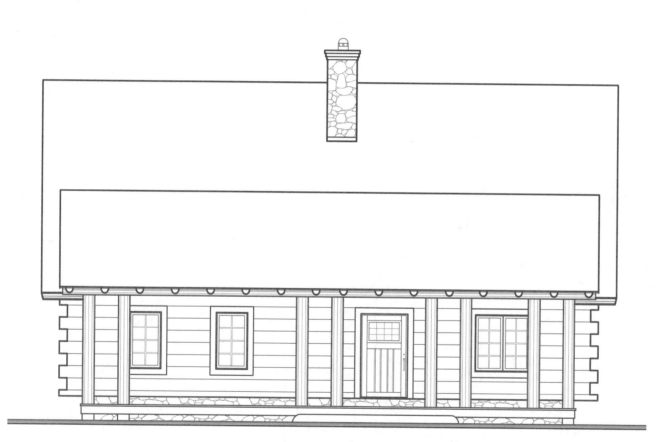

This log home is the perfect getaway camp for the family who requires plenty of extra bedrooms in a very modest footprint. There are a total of five bedrooms and three bathrooms, all incorporated into a cost-effective design. This architect has a great feel for living within a limited size and budget. His understanding and appreciation for New England thrift is evident in this home's design.

The first-floor main entry has a full-length covered porch that says "classic log cabin." From the living area, the focus is the fireplace—all the public space shares a view of the crackling stone fireplace. Tucked into the back of the house are two bedrooms with a shared bathroom.

The second-floor loft has a master bedroom with a study/library perched above the living room below. The bathroom is carved out of the roofline, created by a dog-shed dormer. It has a wonderful window bench built into the wall, with plenty of storage space underneath for linens.

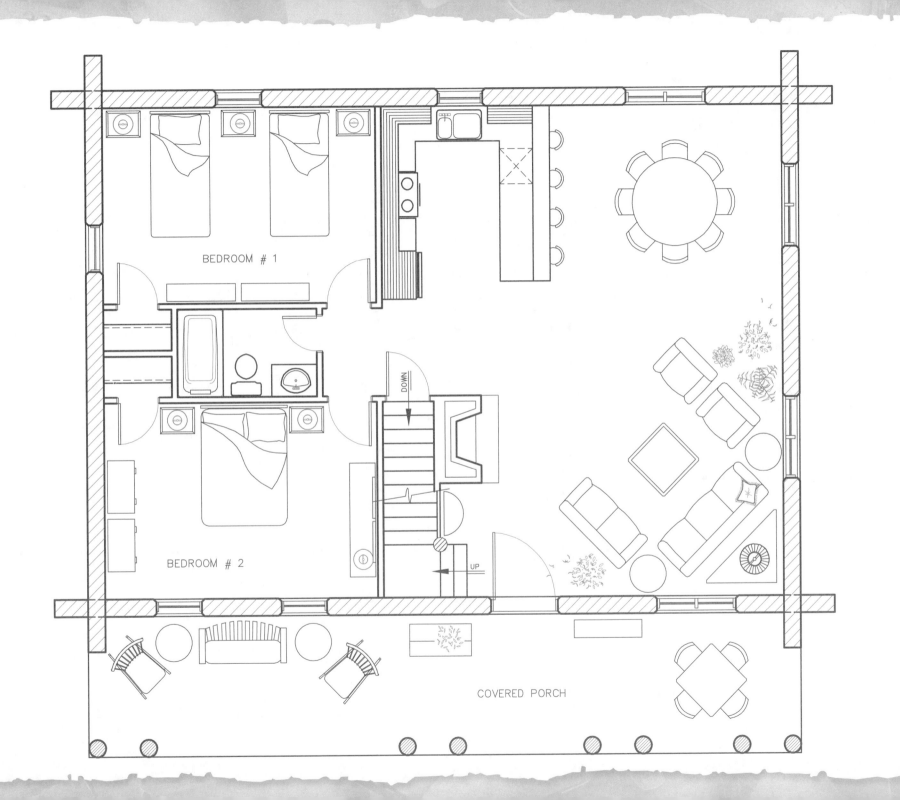

BEDROOM # 1

BEDROOM # 2

DOWN

UP

COVERED PORCH

137

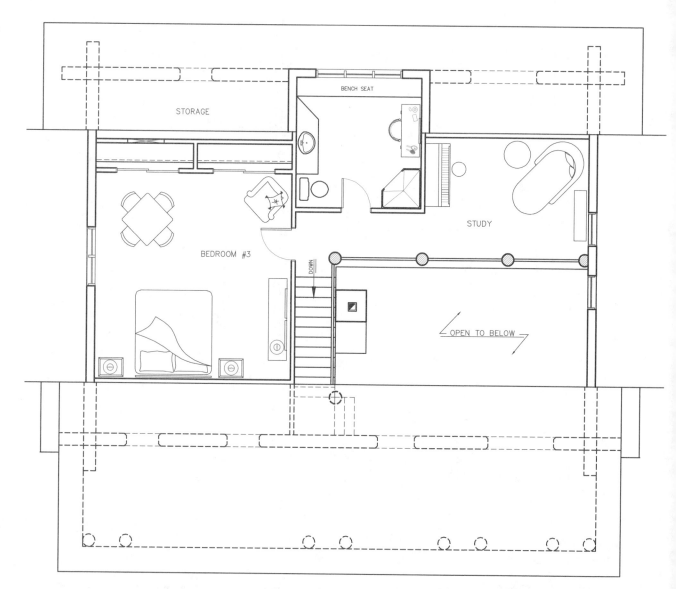

The daylight basement has a fireplace located in the recreation room and plenty of windows for viewing nature. There are two more bedrooms and a full bathroom tucked away downstairs to house even more family and friends.

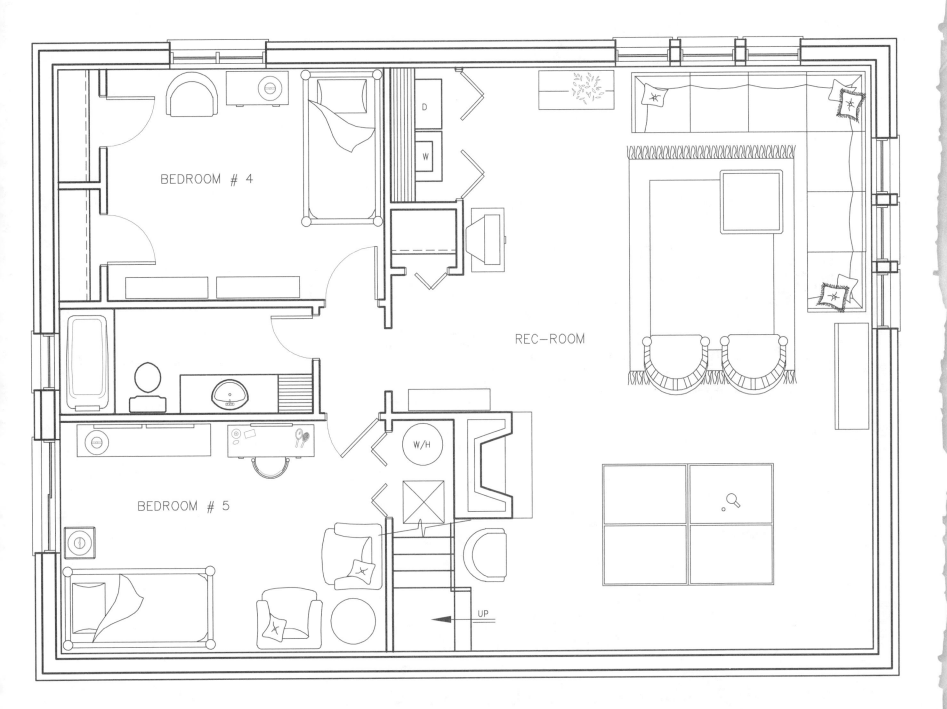

BEDROOM # 4

D

W

BEDROOM # 5

REC-ROOM

W/H

UP

Truckee Lodge

Main Floors: 3,465 square feet

This design incorporates a roof system engineered for heavy snow loads. The additional log purlins add charm to the home's character by creating visual interest. The conventionally built garage and mudroom are thoughtfully blended into the home's design with the use of log elements and a mix of textures that complement the log structure.

A covered porch leads into an air-lock entry, where French doors swing open into the great room with a massive core fireplace that anchors the living area. The living room's conservatory effect is created by a bank of windows that reach from the floor to the ceiling. The large country kitchen has a central work island and peninsula that spills over into a light-filled dining area. Off to one side of the kitchen is the large mudroom with a washer and dryer. The mudroom creates a bridge that connects the garage to the main house.

The first floor has a large recreation/media room with its own private covered porch. A

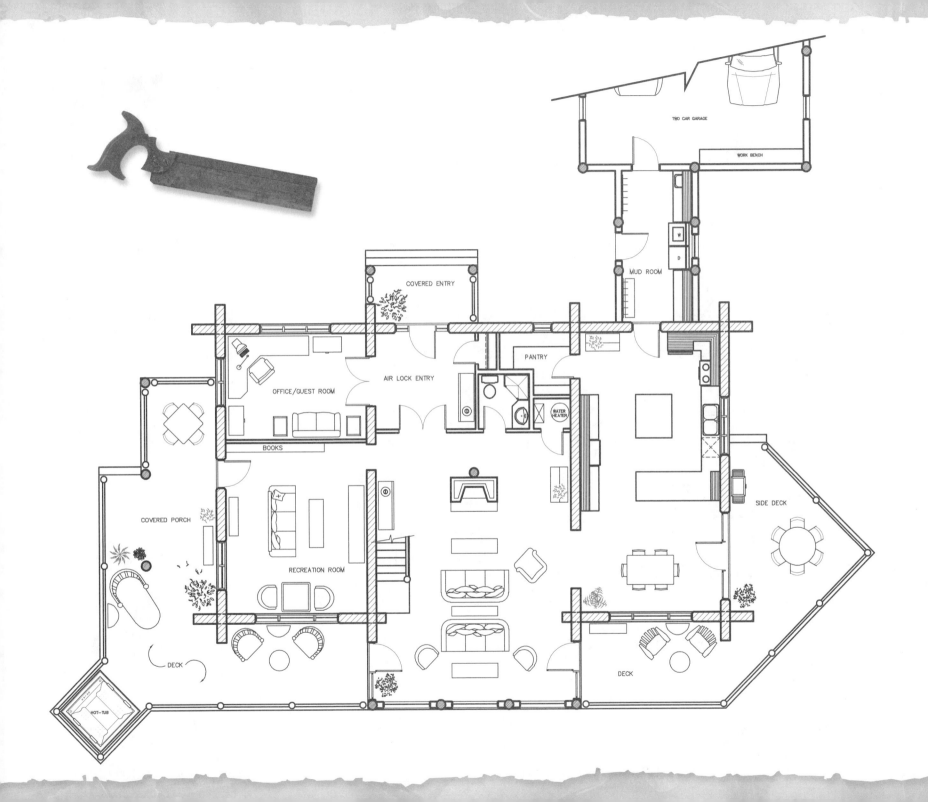

TWO CAR GARAGE

WORK BENCH

W

D

MUD ROOM

COVERED ENTRY

PANTRY

AIR LOCK ENTRY

OFFICE/GUEST ROOM

WATER HEATER

BOOKS

SIDE DECK

COVERED PORCH

RECREATION ROOM

DECK

DECK

HOT-TUB

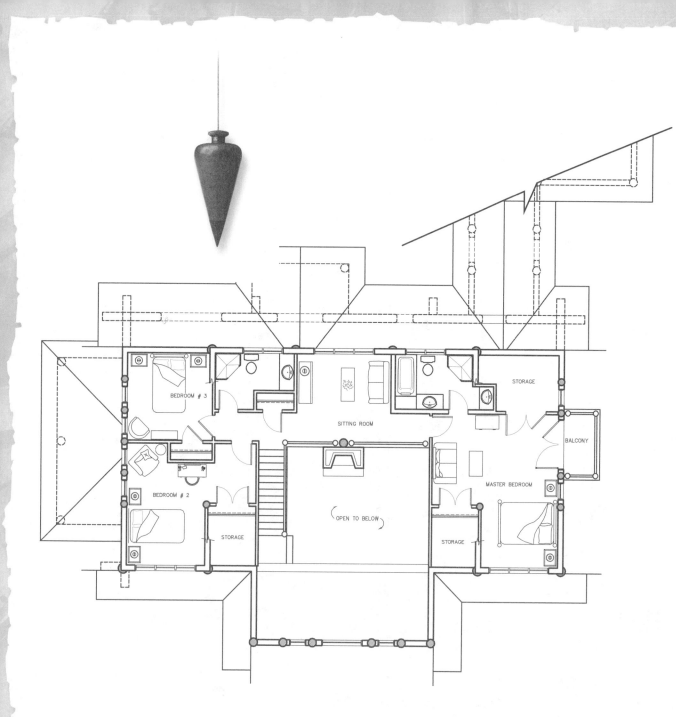

separate office can also double as a guest room for extra family and friends. The second-floor loft connects the two bedroom wings, with a sitting nook set into the shed dormer. There are three bedrooms and two bathrooms located on the second floor. The bump-outs and jogs of the roofline create an artful fluid movement that transforms raw logs into a sculpture of nature.

BEDROOM # 3

STORAGE

SITTING ROOM

BALCONY

BEDROOM # 2

STORAGE

OPEN TO BELOW

MASTER BEDROOM

STORAGE

Nickels Pond

Main Floor: 2,572 square feet

This architect created an L-shaped log home with a fluid movement of space. The rooflines create a covered entry that leads into a large expansive foyer. The open living space is centered around the fireplace. The kitchen has an efficient work triangle with the convenience of a large walk-in pantry.

French doors open into a master bedroom suite with a walk-in closet and plenty of linen storage space within the private bathroom. The two-car garage is seamlessly incorporated into the home's design. There is a laundry that has the convenience of a back door and a mudroom entry, with a washer, dryer, and folding table that can all be closed away once the laundry starts to pile up.

The U-shaped staircase has a graceful midway landing that curls up and away to a second-floor loft, where two more bedrooms share a full-sized bathroom with the added luxury of a soaking tub and separate shower. One of the bedrooms has a wonderful covered balcony that extends the living space, providing an added outdoor room to watch sunsets after a long summer's day.

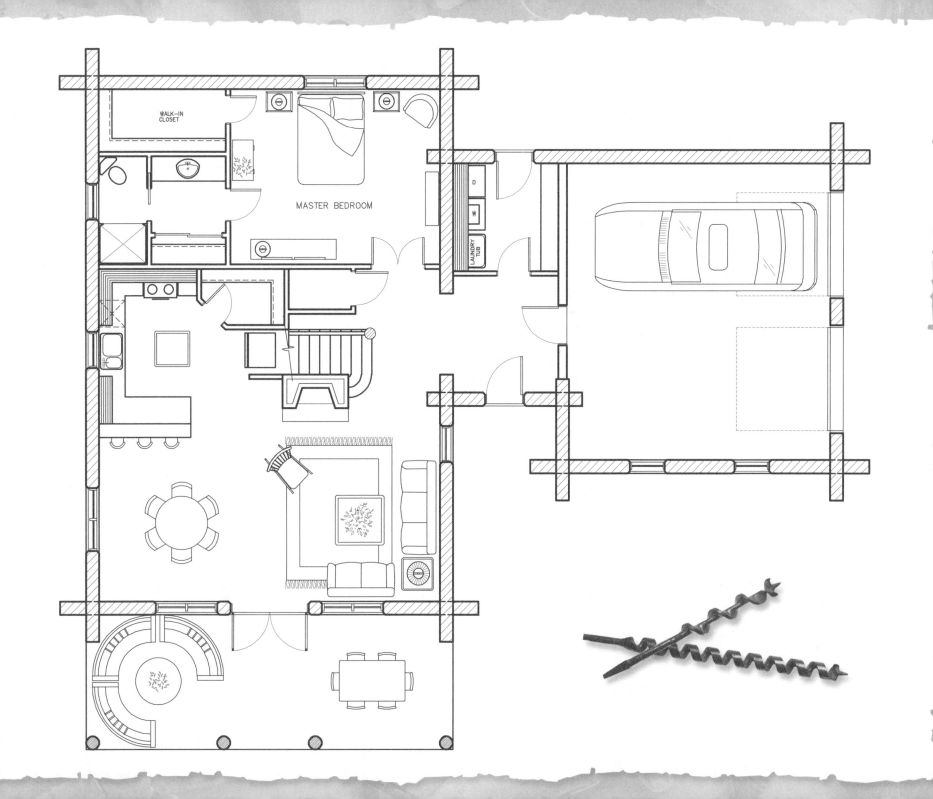

WALK-IN
CLOSET

MASTER BEDROOM

D

W

LAUNDRY
TUB

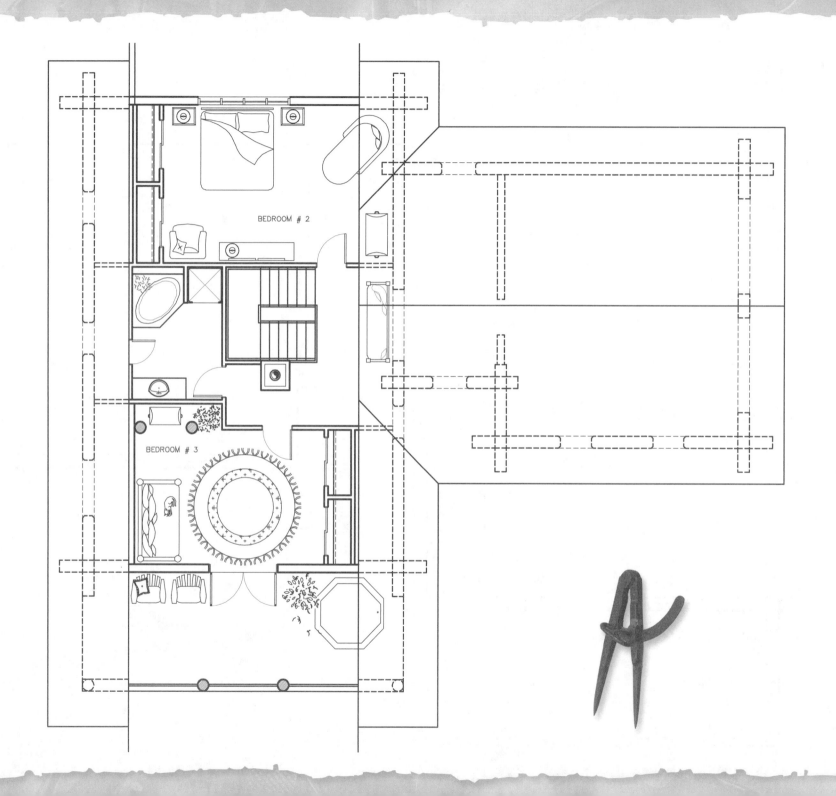

BEDROOM # 2

BEDROOM # 3

146

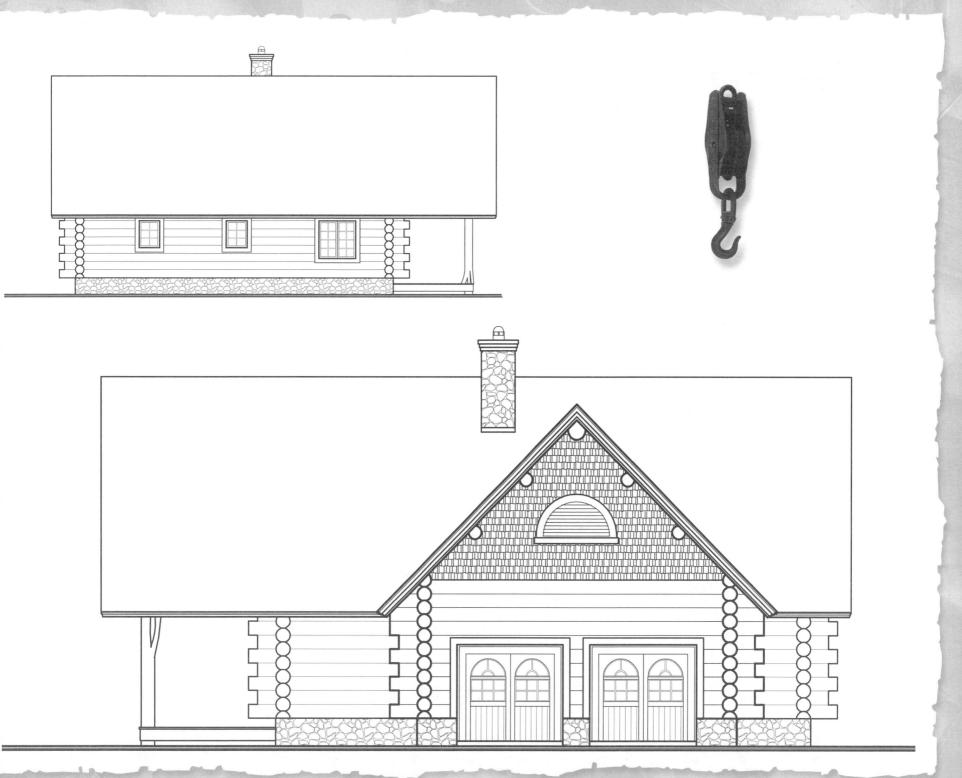

Cabin-on-the-Meadows

Main Floor: 1,280 square feet

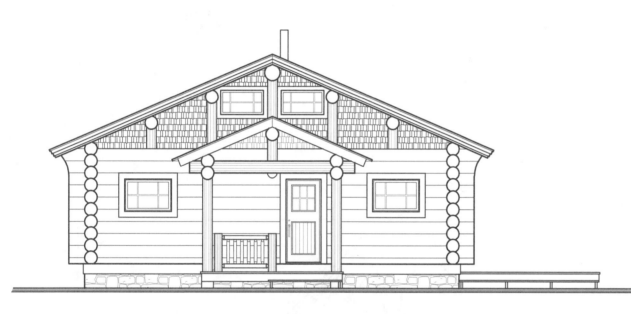

This cabin is carefully planned and wonderfully considered to make the most of its compact size without feeling cramped. The architect's years of experience designing log structures are not only evident in the layouts, but go beyond their design to capture a classic fluid movement. She was very gracious to share the floor plans she originally designed as a contender for her own personal cabin on the meadows.

The entry welcomes you into a comfortable area to take off your shoes. The entry closets help hide and organize all those "loose flying" objects. A small guest room or office on the main level can do double duty as an overnight retreat for family or friends. The primary bedroom is located off the bathroom and laundry. The open space of the living room, dining room, and kitchen create an open airy feel. The large deck is a great extension of the living space for plenty of warm-weather entertainment.

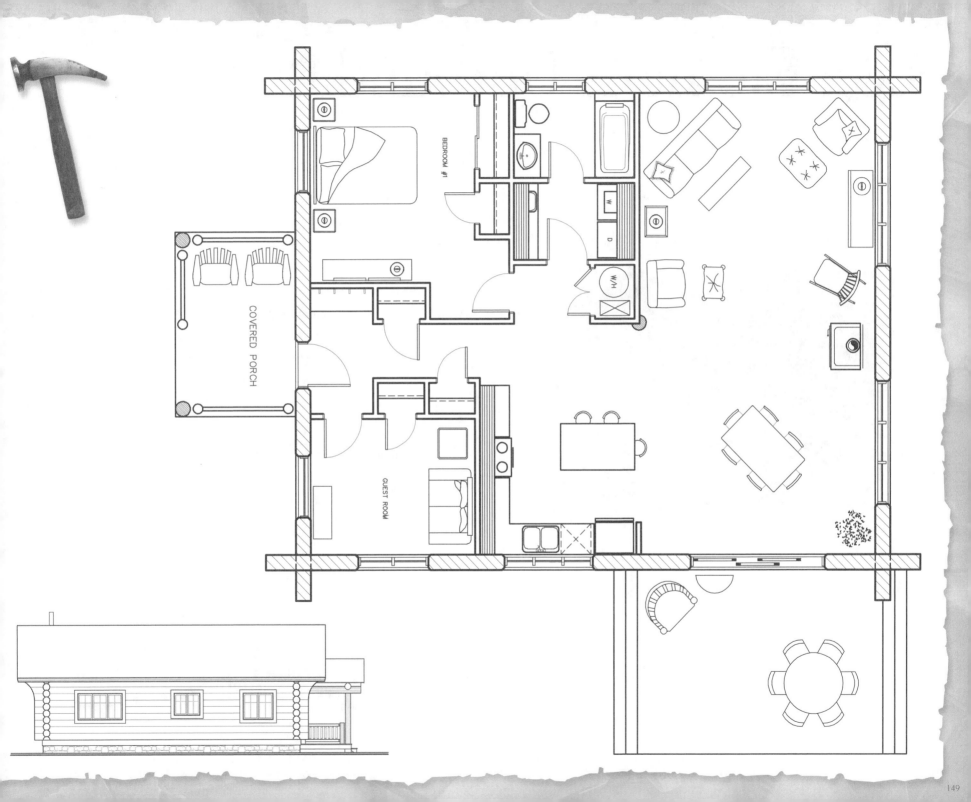

BEDROOM #1

COVERED PORCH

GUEST ROOM

Log Element Outbuildings

This style of a conventional, stick-frame structure incorporates a few log elements, tying the structure's design in with the log home's structure without building more log walls. This form of construction is perfect for the person who wants a separate structure, such as a standard garage, but does not require the added insulation provided by the natural properties of a log wall.

The log element base starts with conventional construction-framing methods enhanced by the use of log elements, "twig art" detailing, and often a kiss of log whimsy. The combination of log elements can be log roof systems, log floor joists, log stairs, log rails, or log support columns within a conventionally built structure. These methods create a dramatic contrast of rustic logs and conventional materials. Log element building is for those who want to incorporate the rustic elements of nature into a conventional stick-frame structure. It can be a mix of the sophisticated cabin style as in the old Adirondack Great Camps built at the turn of the century, while being a bit more casual in feel than the traditional timber-frame structure.

Saltbox Garage

Garage Area: 484 square feet

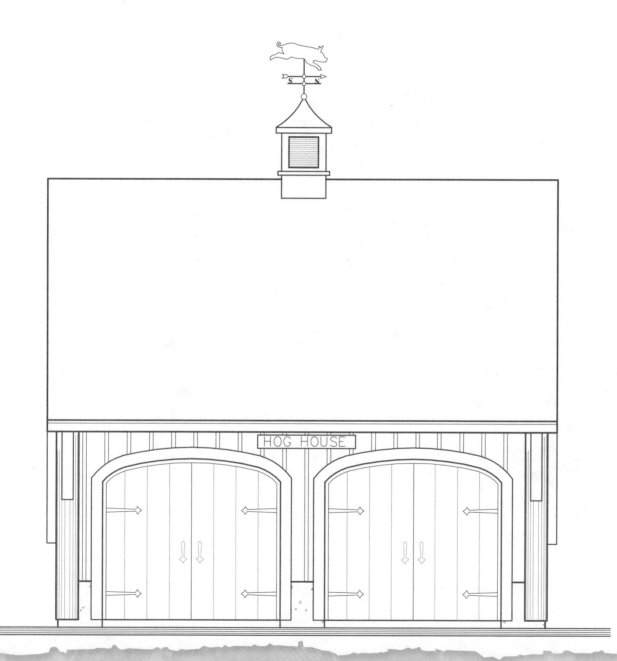

HOG HOUSE

This New England Saltbox roof line has a classic shape. The two-car bay is perfect for additional storage of garden tools, lawn equipment, boat storage, or the perfect cover for the Harley as a comfortable "hog" house (which fits right in with the flying pig weather vane).

The side door allows quick access. Inside there is a pull-down ladder to a small attic storage area. The extended roof line creates a great area for wood storage. The garage doors can be on hinges like a traditional garage or barn door or can be modified and adapted to a one-door unit in combination with an electrical garage door opener. This design is most requested by clients who prefer to have an alternative area in which to retreat.

WOOD STORAGE

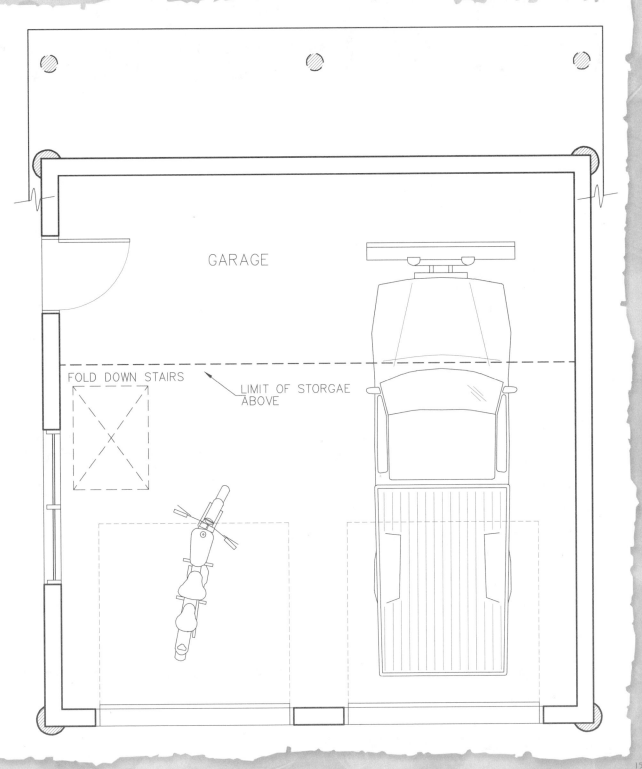

GARAGE

FOLD DOWN STAIRS

LIMIT OF STORGAE ABOVE

Carriage House Garage

Living Area: 680 square feet • Garage Area: 1,700 square feet (two levels)

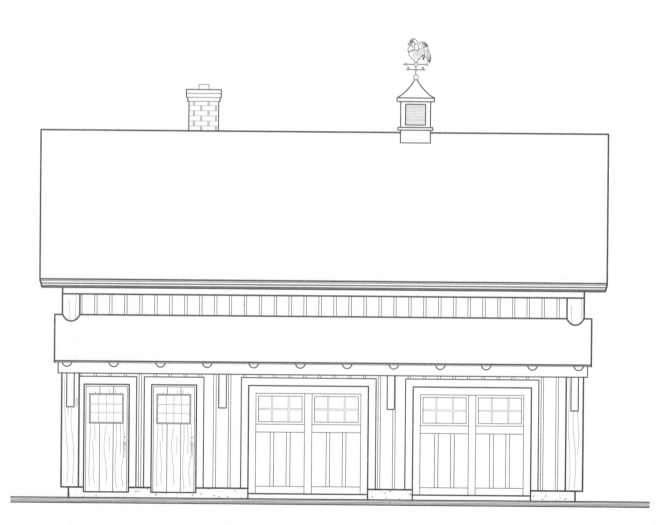

This *carriage house classic even incorporates a caretaker's flat.* There is a two-car bay located on the main floor level with a workbench and shelving. The woodstove is a wonderful addition to the workshop for those long, cold winter projects. Stairs lead to another lower-level garage that takes advantage of a hillside slope that day-lights the lower level garage for added storage of boats, recreational vehicles, snowplows, and heavy equipment, as well as gardening and yard equipment; it can also be modified to suit other needs.

The separate entry door climbs to the upper-level apartment that also has the added warmth of a central woodstove. The living area feels open and spacious. The dine-in kitchen is carved out of the roof system by incorporating a log rafter dormer. The bar-style kitchen has a refrigerator tucked under the counter, along with plenty of additional storage in a walk-in pantry.

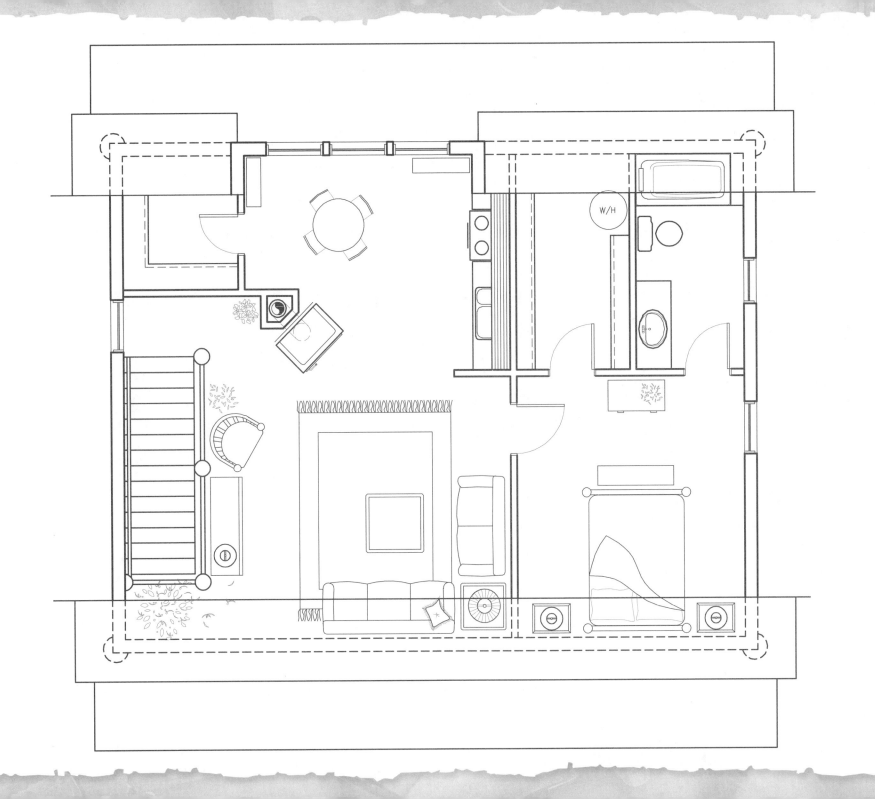

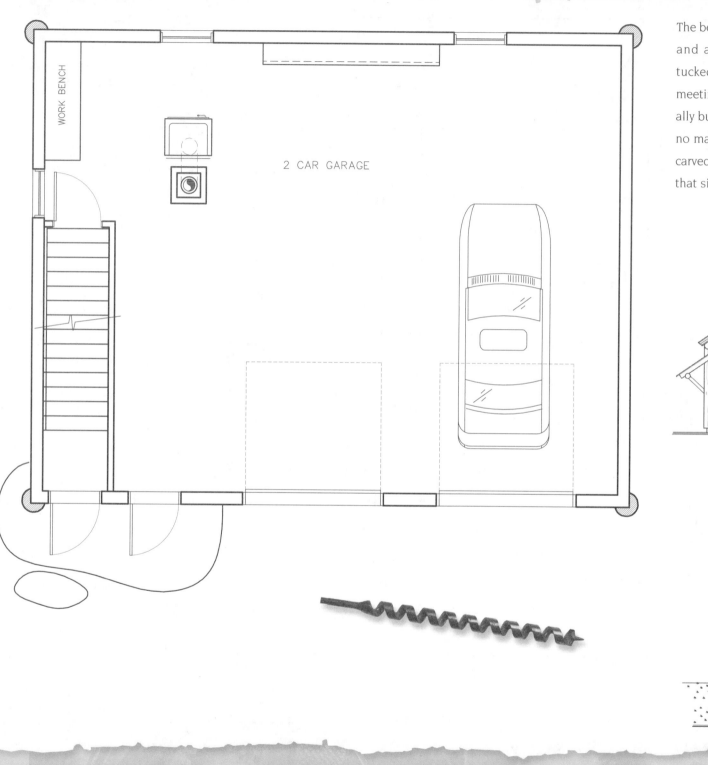

WORK BENCH

2 CAR GARAGE

The bedroom suite has a large walk-in closet and a good-sized bathroom with a tub tucked in under the slope of the roof line meeting the knee wall. The 2 x 6 conventionally built, three-story structure has character no matter what angle it is viewed from. The carved crowing rooster is the crowning touch that sings no matter what the time of day.

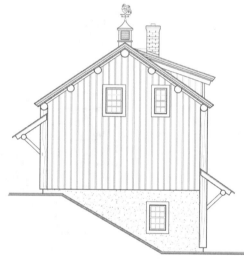

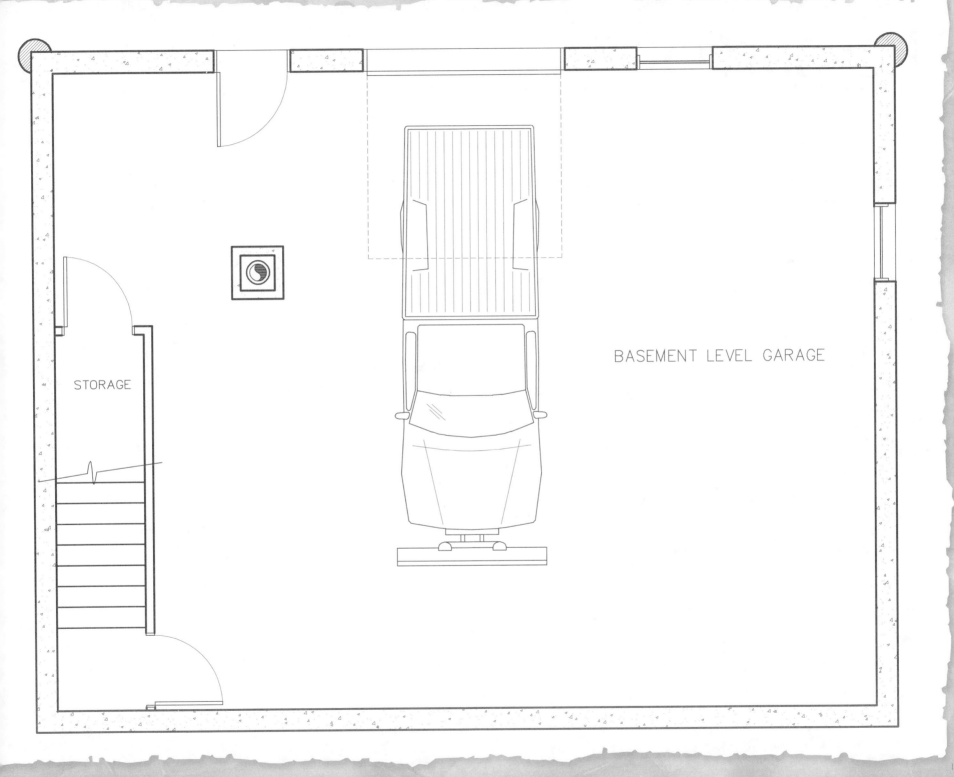

STORAGE

BASEMENT LEVEL GARAGE

Resources

Blueprint Price Information

The plans in this book can be purchased from

Beaver Creek Design Services

35 Territory Road
Oneida, NY 13421
www.beavercreekdesignservices.com
(315) 245-4112

Garage Plans:

    5 Sets $325.00
    8 Sets $375.00

Small Log Cabin Collection
(under 999 sq. ft.):

    5 Sets $485.00
    8 Sets $535.00

Log Home Storybook Collection
(1,000–1,999 sq. ft.):

    5 Sets $745.00
    8 Sets $795.00

Log Home Estate Collection
(2,000–2,999 sq. ft.):

    5 Sets $845.00
    8 Sets $895.00

ALL PRICES ARE SUBJECT TO
CHANGE WITHOUT NOTICE.

All prices are subject to shipping and handling costs. Orders should be made carefully. All plans are specifically printed for each client with no refunds available.

Bead-and-Batten Doors

ATS Inc.

30 East Little Avenue
Driggs, ID 83422
(208) 456-2711
Traditional bead-and-batten and
Z-back–style doors.

The Tree House Troll

Carvings by Hoppy
137 Dewitt Road
Olive Bridge, NY 12461
(845) 626-2052
The most realistic wood carvings of bears, wolves, horses, eagles, and more (photo on pg. 159).

Eagle Panel Systems, Inc.

P.O. Box 247
Mulberry Grove, IL 62262-0247
www.eaglepanelsystems.com
(618) 326-7132
(800) 643-3786
Insulated roof panels with fewer thermal breaks than a conventionally built roof system.

Heartland Appliances

1050 Fountain Street North
Cambridge, ON N3H 4R7
Canada
www.heartlandappliances.com
(800) 361-1517
Wood, electric, and gas stoves, along with built-in ovens with traditional charm.

International Log Building Association

P.O. Box 775
Lumby, BC V0E 2G0
Canada
www.logassociation.org
(250) 547-8776
(800) 532-2900
The Log Building Association Web site lists hundreds of traditional hand-crafters from all over the world. Many listings are never seen within the standard log-building magazines.

Log Home Guide

P.O. Box 671
1107 NW 4th Street
Grand Rapids, MN 55744-0671
www.loghomeguide.com
(888) 345-LOGS [5647]
A special-issue magazine with a hand-selected list of the top one hundred log builders in North America. A valuable resource list of handcrafted log builders within your region.

Nortek Log Home Systems

P.O. Box 118

Pembine, WI 54156-0118

www.jack-wrap.com

(888) 488-2380

Decorative copper skirts that hide
the screw-jack systems in log homes.
All variations of both the round-and-
square style Jack-Wraps are patent-
pending products.

Schroeder Log Home Supply, Inc.

34810 U.S. Hwy 2

Grand Rapids, MN 55744

www.loghelp.com

(800) 359-6614

Specialty products catalog for the log
home (tools, stains, preservatives,
and hardware).

Slatecraft

1796 Apple Valley Drive

Howard, OH 43028

www.slatecraft.com

(740) 393-1716

Slate switch-plate and electrical covers,
handcrafted from weathered slate roof-
ing tiles removed from barns dating
back more than a century.

Tenonizer Technology

10480 Tenonizer Trail

Nissa, MN 56468

(218) 829-9046

www.tenonizer.com

Instructional videos and equipment for
constructing log furniture, handrails,
and stairs (photo on pg. 30).

Wood Window Workshop

839 Broad Street

Utica, NY 13501

(315) 732-6755

(800) 724-3081

Quality, custom-built Craftsman-style
windows. Specializing in old-world style
and in-swing windows with brass
cremone bolts.